THE ROLE OF PROVIDENCE IN
THE SOCIAL ORDER

THE ROLE OF PROVIDENCE
IN THE SOCIAL ORDER

AN ESSAY IN INTELLECTUAL HISTORY

JACOB VINER

Jayne Lectures for 1966

The American Philosophical Society

PRINCETON, NEW JERSEY

PRINCETON UNIVERSITY PRESS

Contents

Foreword

In 1966 Professor Viner was invited to give the Jayne Lectures of the American Philosophical Society. He had long been interested in the relationship between religious doctrines and economic theory and behavior, and in these lectures he presented some of the conclusions that he had reached after years of thoughtful study. He concerned himself especially with the way in which the idea of providence was used to justify existing economic and social conditions. Providence favors trade among peoples in order to promote universal brotherhood; providence also creates social inequality because it is part of the divine plan. These and other ideas he discussed with his usual wit and learning. But lectures are subject to time limitations and Professor Viner could cite only small fragments of the vast body of material that he had accumulated to support his conclusions. He therefore planned to expand the lectures into a longer book and to add the footnotes that would have illustrated the peculiar and unexpected combinations of religious and economic doctrine that appear during the centuries. He spent a great deal of time on this work, but increasing ill-health forced him to slow down his activities. He died in 1970 with the book still incomplete.

We are all the losers by this incompleteness. Everyone who knew Jacob Viner remembers his extraordinary knowledge of books, his ability to find striking ideas in the most unlikely places, his mastery of many fields besides his own. He knew more history than many historians and he delighted in giving new twists to the history of economic thought. The complete book would have touched off a long series of articles and doctoral dissertations.

But we would be equally the losers if the lectures were not published at all. They do distill the results of long and thorough research; they do present ideas that Viner wanted us to discuss. They are incomplete only in the sense of being less inclusive and less well documented than the author wanted them to be. In themselves they are a finished and a polished piece of writing. A master has stated his conclusions; it will be profitable for us to seek his sources and to try to retrace his reasoning.

JOSEPH R. STRAYER

Princeton University

THE ROLE OF PROVIDENCE IN THE SOCIAL ORDER

I. The Cosmic Order in the Service of Man

I AM PRESENTING these lectures to you as merely an exercise in the history of ideas. The particular set of ideas which I will examine relates to the role of providence in the social order as seen, primarily in the seventeenth and eighteenth centuries, by intellectuals in general, and by theologians, philosophers of various species, and economists in particular. Some of these ideas no doubt had a substantial influence on the course of history in these centuries, but as to this I venture no claims. It has been said of the ideas of political philosophers and economists that almost on their own they have ruled the world. Perhaps so. In any case, I have a professional vested interest in believing it to be so. But most of the thinkers I will be dealing with in these lectures would have regarded as impious the idea that the ideas of men, even of men as important as themselves, ruled the world as a final cause. They would have insisted, instead, that it was providence that ruled the world. For the moment, I will defer paying my respects to the role of providence and look only at secondary causes.

There is a theory, which is a quasi-religion for some men and is regarded by perhaps a majority of modern intellectuals as having a large measure of validity, which holds that it is the material circumstances in which men live, and especially the social structure and economic institutions of society which govern the behavior of men, and via practice, shape their thought, including even their thoughts about providence. Karl Marx, in 1843, applied this thesis to religion in his most dogmatic manner: "religious misery is, on one hand, the expression of actual misery, and, on the other, a protest against actual misery. Religion is the sigh of the oppressed creature, the kindliness of a heartless world, the spirit of unspiritual conditions. It is the people's opium."

1

A rival theory is that it is the great men who determine the course of history, the men of action in the material world, the great thinkers in the world of ideas. It is, I suppose, the responsibility of social historians to decide between the competing theories as to the causes and consequences of the ideas which men hold. In any case, as I am not a social historian, I do not accept it as an immediate responsibility of mine, and I will endeavor to remain strictly within the narrow and modest sphere of the history of ideas. This, as I understand it, accepts no responsibilities except those imposed by the standards of scholarly objectivity, whose essence can be summarized in two precepts: first, be as neutral as you can in reporting other men's ideas, yielding neither to favorable nor to unfavorable bias, nor to unmotivated carelessness; second, bear in mind that this, even an approach to accuracy in reporting, is an arduous and difficult art, calling for unintermitting self-discipline.

Objectivity is not an all-purpose virtue. One can, I suppose, pay a higher price for it in surrendered values than it is worth in some circumstances. As it operates in the history of ideas it can result in a lifeless, bloodless, anaemic academic discipline, one which isolates ideas from human minds and passions and treats them as a species of intellectual atoms, as particles of thought which emerged from nothingness and will return to it, causeless and devoid of consequences. It may have no function except that of providing the historian with a vacation from true history of man's thought or providing him with a vocation which furnishes him with subsistence and occasional fun, but leaves him free from the need of making moral or religious or political or economic judgments as part of his professional task. It would be libelous to assert that this is a fair account of how in fact most historians of ideas operate. With minor qualifications, however, I confess that it comes reasonably close to how I have tried to operate when I have

practiced the art of *Ideengeschichte.* In the past I have for
the most part been otherwise engaged, in trying to generate
ideas of my own, or to improve the morals of others, or
either to help rescue contemporary society from the sad
cultural predicament I am told it is in, or to protect society
from its would-be rescuers, or to solve technical economic
problems. The only assistance I was then conscious of
deriving from such knowledge as I had of the history of
ideas was a lesson it taught me with a very close approach
to certainty. Outside the quite extensive area where tautol-
ogy rightly rules, certainty is beyond the reach of man, but
for effectiveness in the life of action the false assurance that
one has attained certainty is easy to achieve and is a great
help and a great comfort.

It is possible however, to make more of the history of
ideas than the mechanical compilation of annals or chron-
icles of autonomous ideas, all free, equal, and of no visible
interest except to those perhaps mythical scholars, the old-
fashioned antiquarians. In relation to the outside world,
including the spheres of thought which use as raw material particular ideas, there are many kinds of ideas and,
with effort, the kinds can in practice be distinguished more
or less precisely from each other. Depending upon time
and place, also, the same idea may be performing in different roles. Given the appropriate knowledge, the observer
may be able in any particular set of circumstances to
identify the role which is dominant for a particular idea,
and thus relate the idea to the thought, the doctrines, the
passions and hopes, the material circumstances, of mankind in that time and place. The idea may be operating
functionally, that is, it may be influencing the behavior of
those who are possessed of or by it, and thus may have
practical consequences. The idea may find use only as a
part of traditional rote, not related logically to its intellectual context, and now playing only a ceremonial role as

a residue of the functional thought of a distant past. The idea may have an aesthetic role, as decoration or ornamentation for an argument or thesis, or as raw material for the poet or dramatist. The idea may be an implement of play, the tennis-ball, so to speak, of an intellectual game which can have strict rules designed to provide standards of skill for players and spectators. Finally, the idea, though dead and functionless, may be an object of innocent curiosity, like uncommon pebbles or ancient artifacts which offer scope for the acquisition of connoisseurship. It is on the basis of some blend of these roles that I accept the history of ideas as a legitimate avocation for myself, but I hope that my audience, with its wider range of skills and interests, and no doubt its more profound convictions, will find in these lectures more solid justification for listening to them than I have the presumption to claim on their behalf.

Providence, as an intelligent being, external to nature but governing nature, is an idea common to most religions. The term, or its equivalent in various languages, is often used also to signify the pattern in which that supernatural being conducts his operations. I will use it in both senses.

In the Christian tradition, especially perhaps in the period I am in these lectures specially concerned with, the seventeenth and eighteenth centuries, a distinction is made on the one hand between "general providence," or God operating through secondary causes, or through the "laws of nature," and on the other hand, "particular" or "peculiar" or "special" or "extraordinary" providence, or God operating directly, either in a special manipulation of the laws of nature, or without reference to the laws of nature, or in direct suppression of them. Somewhere within the range of "particular providence," but not as a rule regarded as embracing its whole range, come "miracles." "Secondary causes" signify the operation of the laws of nature. "Final causes" signify the operations of providence, whether direct, without the mediation of the laws of nature, or indirect, with the mediation of these laws. All causation is thus immediately or ultimately final, except where there is recognized to be a field of operations for the devil, for demons, for false gods, and for witches, sorcerers, evil spirits, and magicians, all these last regarded as agents of the devil.

My particular concern in these lectures is with ideas concerning the role of providence in the temporal social order of mankind. Expressly or by implication in the Judeo-Christian Scriptures, as also in the religious thought of ancient Greece and Rome, there is a special relationship between providence and this earth, and between providence and the human inhabitants of this earth, or of a portion of them, a chosen people, or the portion of mankind which a special revelation has reached, or the faithful among the latter. A good deal of early theological doctrine, Christian and non-Christian, however, was not expressly anthropocentric, or not exclusively so, and was concerned with the relations of providence to the universe as a whole, to this earth as a whole, and to all of its organic life. It was in this area where, by virtue of new observations and discoveries, apparent discrepancies between Biblical texts and observed or reasonably inferrable facts first became important. The first stages of providential doctrine, therefore, gave extensive attention to the relations of providence to the cosmic order, to the physical order. Social thought was primitive and scanty, and while Christianity continued to be a minority and a persecuted cult, without a share in government, it concentrated its thought about humanity on the relations of the indivdual to God and on the City of God which was in prospect, rather than on the problems of communal life in the earthly cities of sinful men.

The general framework of providentialist doctrine thus was set initially largely in terms of the relation of God to the physical order of the cosmos he had created, and on the path to immortal life he had established for mankind. Admiration of the beauties, the regularities, and the magnificence of the cosmic order was primarily a religious act, an act of veneration of God's majesty, and not, as it later sometimes became, an expression of gratitude for temporal benefits which mankind in general derived from the cosmic order.

In the state of knowledge of nature of the early Christians, the account of the cosmic order derivable from Genesis did not conflict with what their naked and untrained eyes could perceive, and presumably left most of them untroubled by doubts as to the reliability of that account. St. Augustine, however, warned the Christians of his time not to make themselves laughable to sophisticated Greeks by presenting their naive notions about matters of fact relating to natural science as resting on the sacred writings when to the Greeks such notions were in direct conflict with propositions which they regarded as demonstrably true on the basis of reason and experience. St. Augustine's primary concern was apparently not to improve the understanding of nature by rank-and-file Christians. Nor is it at all clear that he was conceding that Genesis, properly interpreted, could not be reconciled with the latest findings of Greek science. He did, however, make it reasonably clear that he believed that Genesis was not to be read literally as a reliable treatise on scientific matters. Christians, he said, should be prudent, restrained, and if possible well-informed in using the Scriptures for exposition of matters on which scientific testimony was relevant and available; if they acted otherwise, it would impair their efficacy as expounders of the Christian faith to the unconverted. I have failed to find that this advice of St. Augustine had any direct influence on later theologians or ecclesiastics. In any case, it seems to be the fact that it was those branches of the Christian faith which departed most widely from the Augustinian tradition who were most receptive to innovations in science and went furthest in accommodating their theology to the findings of scientists.

The early Christians were largely recruited from among the poorer classes. There was little occasion for them to be grateful to a kind providence which showered them with temporal blessings. In any case, it was not worldly ease and prosperity which they were taught to expect from Christianity, but hope for happiness in a future life. The doctrines of the Fall of Man and of the Flood, and of their adverse consequences for the material state of mankind on this earth and even for the physical state of the earth itself, called for a pessimistic and not an optimistic view of the relations of the physical cosmos to man's temporal welfare. What has been called the "Christian optimism" of early Christianity was in any normal sense of the term "optimism" only such with respect to the prospects for an idyllic afterlife, and even these prospects were often held to be dim for many, perhaps for most, of the believers. The new optimism of the seventeenth century and later, which was to have an important impact on social thought, was in part a turning away from the Augustinian tradition in Christianity and from the doctrine of original sin. It was in part even a turning away, in the guise of "deism," from revealed religion.

In the Old Testament there are occasional references to the benefits man derives from the firmament, the "heavens"; they provide mankind with rain, with the succession of the seasons, with the alteration of cold and warmth, and with favorable winds. St. Paul (Romans, 1.20) cited the understanding that man gets of the nature of God from what is visible of the universe that he created, and St. Augustine later relied heavily on this text to justify inferences as to the nature of God from what we know of the universe he created. The appeal to the order that reigns throughout the universe as evidence of design and therefore of the existence of the gods had been made in Greece, at least as early as the seventh century B.C. as an argument against the doctrine that the universe was the product of chance.

The use of the argument from design for demonstrating the existence of God does not appear to have become widespread until the seventeenth century. It, of course, constituted the *Via Quinta* of the famous effort of St. Thomas Aquinas to prove the existence of God philosophically; that is, without appeal to revelation. Until, however, there existed widespread skepticism or doubt about the authority of the Scriptures, there was not much occasion for seeking support for belief in God's existence from philosophy or science or human reason.

The first of the great threats to the credibility of the Biblical account of the origin and mode of operation of the physical universe emanating from scientific discovery was, of course, the Copernican revolution in astronomy in the sixteenth century. The establishment of the theory that the earth rotated daily on its axis and that the planets, including the earth, revolved in orbits around the sun, seemed to some to constitute a major rejection of the geocentric interpretation of the universe which the Scriptures expounded; the heliocentric doctrine threatened the authority of a theology based on a historical account of miraculous events occurring in a small corner of a small planet in an infinite universe. Development of the argument from design as a support of belief in the existence of an all-powerful supernatural being became for the first time since the establishment of the Christian faith an urgent necessity for those believers who were acquainted with the progress of scientific thought.

The Copernican shock to traditional theology was of

course only the first of a continuing series. Geological discoveries which tended to cast doubt on the credibility of the world, and still more of the universe, being created in six days and on the age of the world being limited to something under 6,000 years; the beginnings of scrutiny of the inner harmony and the historical authenticity of the Biblical texts in the form in which they had been handed down; much later, the appearance of evolutionary theories and the gradual accumulation of scientific evidence which seemed to support them, all of these were additional landmarks of the growth of speculation and evidence threatening the authority of Scriptures with respect to the physical nature of the universe, and even casting a measure of doubt on its over-all authority. Except for express evolutionary doctrine, whose day was still to come, it was the formidable task of the orthodox theology of the seventeenth century to meet these various challenges to its validity.

The seventeenth and eighteenth centuries met these challenges to traditional beliefs in a variety of ways. The easiest way was to ignore them, or perhaps more precisely, to remain ignorant of them; this was in fact the path taken by many, automatically by the unlearned, more deliberately by others. It would be interesting to know, for instance, how extensive and how protracted was the failure on the part of men of some intellectual status to show in their references to astronomical matters any awareness of what Copernicus, or later Galileo, had said on these matters. I am sure that the experts could readily find instances of such lags exceeding a century. Another way was for ecclesiastics, in the interest of protecting their flocks from disturbance of their traditional beliefs, to coerce or frighten scientists into deferment of publication of their findings, or to extort public retraction of their findings, or even to burn a scientist or two at the stake *pour encourager les autres.*

I have encountered the opinion expressed by a historian

of science that persecution of the scientists did not in fact retard significantly the progress of "science," that is, of scientific propositions which present-day scientists accept as established. That may be so. To make it plausible to me, however, I would have to be persuaded either that "true" science began only yesterday, or that many scientists had a subconscious craving for martyrdom so that the risk of persecution operated as a stimulus instead of a deterrent to dangerous inquiry, or that we possess some scientific technique for discovering the quantity and quality of the scientific inquiries whose results were never disclosed or of inquiries which were abandoned before completion because of fear of persecution. On the law of chances, I should think that the constraints on scientific investigation and publication must have operated to retard the dissemination both of some measure of scientific nonsense and error and some measure of valuable knowledge.

Another way of meeting the new challenges to traditional beliefs arising from new scientific discoveries was to fight the innovators with their own weapons; that is, to expose their scientific error, and to find new scientific supports for old doctrines. This was an important activity in seventeenth- and eighteenth-century England for men of pretensions to scientific expertise. Much nonsense written in the language of science resulted therefrom. But it seems also that some genuine contributions to knowledge also resulted, *per accidentem,* from these investigations. In any case, there seems to be no law of nature which guarantees that the outcome of investigation or experiment carried on with pious bias will not be new and valuable knowledge.

The most important way, however, in which theologians adjusted themselves to scientific innovations was to adapt, or to use the technical term, to "accommodate," their theology to the new information. The most orthodox way of doing so was to apply the traditionally highly elastic and traditionally respectable art of exegesis to the Biblical texts so as to blunt or eliminate any contradiction by these texts, when taken literally, of new information whose claims to validity it was difficult or even for good theological reasons undesirable to impugn. In England in the seventeenth and eighteenth centuries, moreover, there was being expounded a doctrine of so-called "progressive revelation," a term which was used in several different senses. In one sense, it merely liberalized the scope of orthodox exegesis; it treated revelation as immutable, but held that there could be progressive understanding of it. In another sense, the most common one, progressive revelation signified the historical progress from the Old Testament to the New, with a later text canceling in effect an earlier one with which it was in actual or seeming conflict. This was a new formulation of what had been orthodox doctrine from the Christian Fathers. A third meaning of the term, however, involved a more-or-less general license to reject particular Biblical texts instead of merely reinterpreting them, for it postulated the possibility and even probability that new revelation had occurred since the age of the Apostles, that there may indeed have been a continuing revelation, which went beyond the textual contents of the Bible, however interpreted.

For Roman Catholicism, the Church was the exclusive authoritative custodian of the truth, which had when needed infallible access to new light and exclusive authority to validate it, and had never committed itself to the text of the Scriptures and to reason as its sole resource. For it, therefore, the doctrine of progressive revelation in any of its meanings would not have been revolutionary or dangerous doctrine. In the nineteenth century, in fact, something very close to it was formally expounded within the Church, first by Jean-Adam Moehler in Germany, and later by Cardinal

Newman in England, under the label of "development," and seems to have received wide acceptance in Catholic circles.

In Protestantism the situation was different. It had no central church authority as the custodian of doctrine. It made no claims to continuing ecclesiastical access to direct inspiration. It put great emphasis on the rights of individual judgment as to what was true doctrine. Enthusiastically followed, the doctrine of progressive revelation in the third sense I have distinguished—license to reject particular Biblical text instead of merely reinterpreting them—would have opened the way to undisciplined acceptance of innovations in theology. Incidentally, it could in effect have operated to remove all barriers to accommodation of doctrine to new discoveries in science, or to new insights in ethics. It obtained some measure of explicit acceptance in both Anglicanism and Dissent. It is implied in much of English eighteenth-century theological writing. But it never seems to have become "orthodox" in any Protestant religious body with old institutional antecedents.

What was probably the most important factor in facilitating accommodation in seventeenth- and eighteenth-century England between theology and science was a marked shift of emphasis in the theology of both Anglicanism and Dissent from Biblical texts to "natural theology" or to deism, with reason and sentiment in both cases offered as the bases for belief. This shift had many roots: the influence of the Enlightenment in general; disillusionment on humanitarian grounds with much of the Augustinian tradition; the development of a secular ethics resting on human experience instead of traditional dogma, and so forth.

"Natural theology" was not an innovation. It had been freely accepted in Catholicism from at least the late Middle Ages as a supplement to and reinforcement of revealed doctrine. It found early acceptance in Anglicanism. From

1660 on it was the major substance of sermons and treatises in English non-Calvinist Dissent. Although in English theology also, natural theology was in principle only a supplement to and not a corrective of revealed doctrine, in much of eighteenth-century English theological writing the "natural" theology is much more prominent than the "revealed" theology. "Deism" is difficult to define. The word was more often used as an epithet by those hostile to it than as an acceptable label by those friendly to it. Two species of deists can be distinguished: first, those who in their writings systematically abstracted from revelation, or made only token appeals to it, but never explicitly rejected it as unauthentic or of little weight; second, those, sometimes called "critical deists," who more or less openly rejected revealed doctrine, and were suspected, sometimes rightly, as not regarding themselves as Christians. As between moral theologians, non-critical deists, and critical deists, it is rarely easy to be sure of proper classification of any particular individual. Deists were, in fact, often suspected not only of being non-Christians but of being atheists. But if there were any authentic atheists of any consequence in seventeenth- or eighteenth-century England, or Scotland, they were so secretly, and their secret has been kept.

I shall for the time being disregard the Calvinists, as well as Augustinians who did not accept the Calvinist label, for they represent a special case with respect both to their providential doctrines and their attitudes towards science, and therefore can be most conveniently treated separately. As for the others, what basis existed for tension between their religious beliefs and the findings of scientists? As I see it, there were only two that were of major importance, not only for thinking about the physical order of the universe but also for thinking about its moral and social order.

Believers in the full authority of Biblical texts, as literally interpreted, even when these texts expressly or by implication involved propositions about the physical nature of the universe or of any part of it, would be profoundly disturbed by reports of observations by scientists which were in obvious contradiction of such propositions. In practice, as far as intellectuals were concerned, this affected chiefly a minority, and apparently a steadily shrinking one, of conservative Anglicans; other Anglicans could "accommodate" without embarrassment to most new scientific knowledge by resort to established methods of exegesis of Biblical texts. All believers, even if critical deists are included under this designation, would object to propositions expressing or implying the non-existence of a ruling providence which was in some significant sense sovereign over the universe. To many believers, including deists, any account of the universe, or of any portion of it, which pictured it both as not having had a definite time of origin and as being self-operating would seem a denial of any role to providence, and therefore as being offensive on religious grounds.

If this is accepted, and if we continue to defer consideration of Calvinist thought, it is misleading to speak of tensions between religious beliefs and scientific beliefs as to the physical nature of the universe as if they were clear-cut tensions between, on the one hand, the thinking of professional theologians and, on the other hand, the thinking of men addicted to speculation about and investigation of natural phenomena. In the first place, these were often the same men, so that whatever tension was present was internal. In the second place, the Genesis account of the creation of the world and of its subsequent mode of operation was defended, and was rejected, by both professional theologians and professional scientists. The burden of defense, in fact, was too difficult technically to be prudently undertaken by theologians who were merely theologians. It was predominantly persons with pretensions at least to professional competence as scientists, both clerics and laymen, who assumed that burden. In the third place, there was dispute about the manner in which scientific findings should be presented, in which professional theologians and scientists were participants together on *both* sides of the controversy. Such dispute did not necessarily involve difference either in religious beliefs or in the religious implications of the findings of scientists. It could be primarily a dispute about professional manners.

Many scientists protested that their investigations would be hampered if in their scientific work and in the form in which they presented their findings they would be under obligations at every step to trace the sequence of causes from the secondary or immediate causes they were dealing with all the way back to the ultimate or final cause. Many other scientists, on the other hand, after saying what they found to say about the mode of operation of secondary causes indulged freely in dicta or in speculation about the links between the secondary causes and the final cause, or causes. Many pious persons, including scientists, were fearful lest concentration on secondary causes without reference to final causes would give the impression that God was an absent God, who perhaps had once created the universe but, if so, thereafter left it to its own devices as a self-operating machine. Some of them, moreover, saw in the concentration of many scientists on the "order" and regularity of natural phenomena, on the search for "laws of nature," the regrettable result that the general public would interpret their findings in such a manner as to impugn the sovereignty of God, and to leave no room for intermittent or continuous interventions of providence, including both interventions to support the regularity of operation of the laws of nature and interventions by way of miracles to bring about their temporary and partial suspension. But once more, these were concerns of some scientists as well as of some theologians.

Some of the turns which discussion of the relations of theology with science took can be conveniently illustrated by the history of the metaphor of God as a watchmaker, or earlier, as a clockmaker. Its first use has been attributed to a number of writers: among them, Paley, Bolingbroke, Boyle, Sir Walter Raleigh, in England; Fontenelle, Descartes, on the Continent. It goes much further back, however. I can vouch for two fourteenth-century uses of it. It has been attributed to Epictetus. It is to be found in Cicero, not an anachronism, I hasten to say, if any time-measuring device is covered by the term "clock." Its main function has been to illustrate the doctrine that the world, or the universe, by the regularity and order of its operations, demonstrates that it is, like a clock, the product of an intelligent designer, with the clockmaker representing God. It can thus be used as support for an argument for the existence or the skill of God. It can also be used to illustrate the manner of operation of providence with respect to the world, but here it can give rise to serious questions.

Isaac Newton gave a picture of a natural order working with great regularity and efficiency. It had one flaw, however; it needed an occasional special intervention of God to keep it in order. For his friend, Richard Bentley, as for others, this concession that the world once created was not completely self-operating thereafter, but remained dependent upon God, was a necessary and convincing barrier to mechanistic explanations of the universe which left no further role for God once he had created it.

To Leibnitz the Newtonian concession of the necessity for intermittent or periodic intervention by God to support the maintenance of order and regularity in the cosmos was an affront to the workmanship of God in his original design of it. God, he conceded, did make particular interventions, that is perform miracles. This he did, however, not to meet the needs of the physical order but from considerations of grace. In a letter commenting on the system of Newton and his followers, Leibnitz remarked: "According to this doctrine, God Almighty wants to wind up his watch from time to time. Otherwise it would cease to go. God had not, it seems, sufficient foresight to make it a perpetual motion."

Most of the English Newtonians of the eighteenth century quietly omitted from their systems any express provision, such as Newton had made, for occasional providential interventions to keep the cosmos in order. Like Leibnitz they preferred a perpetual motion account of the order of nature. But unanimity on this issue has never prevailed, unless our modern scientists have reached it among themselves. Until at least the end of the eighteenth century, in any case, men were not agreed as to whether providence was an abstaining or an intervening one, whether nature did or did not need help from outside itself in order to maintain its order and regularity, and even whether, with or without the aid of providence, nature was in fact completely orderly and regular. It is interesting that of two contributors to the Jesuit *Journal de Trévoux*, one in 1703 and the other in 1728, both of them using the clock metaphor, one of them professed a preference for the Leibnitzian system of a non-intervening providence, while the other argued that even more irregularity in the operation of the universe than Newton conceded would be required if God were to have adequate scope for free exercise of his sovereignty and expression of his temperament.

Religious thought seems always to have had a natural tendency to find a special place for man in the universe as designed and ruled by providence, that is, to be anthropomorphic. Less universally, but often, it has throughout the ages attributed to man a favored place in the thought of God, not only in the provision of a blissful heaven for the afterlife of such men as receive God's saving grace, but also in the blessings flowing to man from providence in his life on this earth. This I shall label the "optimistic" strain in religious thought. There was also a pessimistic strain, to which I have already had occasion to refer, and to which I shall return later in this lecture. At this point I shall deal with the optimistic strain, as evidenced by the citation of special benefits flowing to man from a physical universe providentially designed, although not necessarily exclusively designed, to serve mankind in his life on this earth.

It seems somewhat paradoxical that the optimistic strain in the Christian tradition grew in strength and reached its greatest dimensions after rather than before the heliocentric system replaced in the minds of at least intellectually sophisticated men the geocentric system which had universally been accepted from ancient times, and which is dominant in the Scriptures. "The heliocentric system," Cassirer has written, "deprived man of his privileged condition. He became, as it were, an exile in the infinite universe." "Man," another author has recently written, "has now lost the illusion that the earth [i.e., man's temporal home] occupies a central and privileged place in the cosmos." This may be true of sophisticated and secularized scientists. I see few traces of evidence that it represents accurately the feelings and beliefs of the mass of mankind in the post-Copernican ages of belief, or even that it would be confirmed today by an objectively designed questionnaire answered by that substantial proportion of mankind in the western world which still maintains affiliations with religious institutions. These two writers, and the many others who have made similar generalizations, underestimate, I believe, the tough shell with which nature, or perhaps providence, has endowed the mind of man so that it resists stubbornly the undermining of its inherited beliefs by the progressive accumulation of scientific knowledge which rebuts ancient notions of the physical nature of the cosmos. Hobbes was once rebuked for thinking that he could make and break monarchies by geometry. If we are prudent, we should perhaps guard against overestimating the power of astronomical knowledge over men's minds and behavior.

In the seventeenth and eighteenth centuries, in any case, it was for many men psychologically impossible to believe that God did not constantly have man in his providential care, and that the physical order of the cosmos was not one of the tools he had designed to serve that purpose. The period in fact abounded, as never before, and perhaps never since, in attempts to demonstrate the manner in which the cosmos served man, much of it written by men with as good claims to be regarded as scientists as any men of their time. Many of these writings today engender chiefly smiles on the part even of laymen ignorant with regard to science, and I suppose that, if today's accredited scientists were to read them, which I am sure they rarely do, they would in the main respond with boisterous laughter. But I am engaged in a venture in objective history, not in an exercise in value judgments, and I know that this literature, while it did arouse some covert ridicule from a few contemporaries, was on the whole warmly received, often ran into many editions, was translated into the leading languages of the western world, and was still being reprinted in the nineteenth century.

The demonstration of the benefits to mankind flowing from the physical structure and mode of operation of the universe external to our sphere was perhaps the most difficult of the tasks undertaken by those who expounded in anthropocentric terms the skill of God's workmanship. Some points could be made easily. It was from the heavens that the nourishing rains came, the rotation of day and night, warmth and coolness when needed by pastures and crops, and so forth. The beauty of the skies brought pleasure to the observant human beings. Even the occasional disturbances of the normal regularity of the outer spheres were often considered particular providences to serve mankind's needs. Philo of Alexandria had already in the first century A.D. shown one way to interpret irregular occurrences, whether on earth or above. Storms, earthquakes, pestilences, served as needed purges of the wickedness of men, and incidentally benefited in various ways those who were not their victims. Some of the early Christian Fathers provided the seventeenth- and eighteenth-century writers on the beneficence of providence with much usable material. Increase Mather in New England expounded the serviceability to mankind of the signs in the heavens. These gave man awareness of the passage of time and upon occasion acted as special warnings that important events were imminent. He interpreted the eclipse in Boston in August, 1672, as evidence that nature shared with Harvard the grief at the death of President Chauncey. Bishop William King, a pioneer contributor to the systematic literature of theodicy, or the optimistic justification to man of the ways of providence, had argued, late in the seventeenth century, that without "peculiar providences" there would be no use in prayer. Edmund Law, his editor, pointed out that this could be used against the preestablished-harmony doctrine of Leibnitz, which denied the need for particular providences to support the normal course of nature. By this time Leibnitz was no longer there to reply, but his answer could have been that he could adhere to his doctrine without conceding the uselessness of prayer by regarding prayer as a method for inducing God to exercise special graces outside of and with no influence on the regular order of nature.

One should not expect to find much in the literature of the period on what service to mankind could be rendered by such spheres as were so distant from this earth that even with the aid of the telescope they could only be dimly per-

ceived. In any case, after some search, my failure to find
such material has been practically complete. One imagina-
tive writer, Robert Jenkin, writing in 1700, did speculate
that if it were to be found that some planets were habitable
but not actually inhabited, this should not be taken as evidence that in the design of providence they were not intended to serve mankind.

> For they might be designed, if mankind had continued in inno-
> cency, as places for colonies to remove men to as the world should
> be increased, either in reward to those that had excelled in virtue
> and piety, to entertain them with the prospect of new and better
> worlds, and so by degrees, to advance them in proportion to their
> deserts, to the height of bliss and glory in heaven; or as a necessary
> reception for men (who would then [that is, before the Fall of
> Man] have been immortal) after the earth had been full of
> inhabitants. . . . And in the meantime, being placed at their
> respective distances, they do by their several motions contribute
> to keep the world at a poise, and the several parts of it at an
> equilibrium in their gravitation upon each other, by Sir Isaac
> Newton's principles.

Isaac Watts, the hymn writer, incidentally seeking a purpose that could be served by all the misery in the world
resulting from original sin, suggested that such misery
might be acting as a useful lesson to populations of other
planets. This is the only instance I know of a writer discussing possible flows of benefits from this earth outwards.

The exponents of an optimistic providentialism possessed, or could acquire, a much greater stock of factual
data, of hypotheses, and of plausible conjectures in their
search for evidence of design favorable to man, when they
studied man's immediate physical environment than when
they studied the stars. They did exploit the resources of
knowledge then available to them in the disciplines of geol-
ogy, botany, zoology, anatomy, physical geography, and
so on, and they worked systematically to acquire new
knowledge, for both its own sake and to serve their pious

purposes. Some used their findings to defend, usually selectively, the account of the physical universe given in Genesis. All inquirers claimed to have discovered new evidence of God's skill as a designer of the universe, and of the eminent fitness of this design to serve the needs of man.

For those who accepted Genesis with some approach to literal interpretation, looking at man's physical environment through rose-tinted spectacles would not have been appropriate. According to Genesis, man because of his sinfulness was to live on this earth subject to various penalties impairing not only his social relations but also his physical environment. Most of the providential writers, however, managed either to interpret the effects of the fall of man in mitigated fashion or largely or wholly to disregard the doctrine of the fall and all or most of the traditional elaboration of the consequences of original sin. The scientific writings of the seventeenth and eighteenth century, with the exception of those of a small group of authors, mostly English, who were largely treated by their contemporaries as morbid pessimists and "enthusiasts," were overwhelmingly optimistic in intent and in the character of their findings. They found evidences of design wherever they looked, and to a large extent they presented these evidences as demonstrating that the design was such as to be beneficial to mankind in its life on earth. If in particular instances they experienced failure to find such evidence, they rarely reported it.

The kinds of evidence of design the scientists most earnestly searched for and were most successful in finding were the fitness of physical environment to the vegetable and animal life existing there, the fitness of organic structure to its function, and finally the serviceability of all this to the needs of mankind. Only rarely did they encounter skeptical questions, sometimes coming from rival scientists who had their own collections of evidence of design. Were, for instance, particular physical environments designed for the convenience of particular plant or animal life, or did the plants and animals wander in search of environments fit for their needs? One type of objection was common; what was the virtue of the fitness of a forest to the needs of an animal dangerous to man, or what the virtue of topographical or climatic conditions fit for the propagation of insects pernicious to animals or to man? One pattern of answer appealed to the chain-of-beings doctrine, which pointed to the virtues of variety—that is, no missing links in the chain—and plenitude—that is full quantitative representation of each link. With the aid of the chain-of-beings doctrine the existence of pernicious insects could be reconciled with the doctrine that this is the best of all possible worlds; after all, these insects also had claims on providence. Or their existence could be justified on the ground of their constituting the food of other animals, or of their beauty. F. C. Lesser, author of a book on insects with the interesting title of *Insecto-Theologia*, first published in 1738, with many subsequent editions and translations, in one chapter heralded even "the devastations made by insects" as "so many marks of the power, the justice, the wisdom, and even of the goodness of God." But without any explanation of his change of approach, his immediately following chapter was an essay on "The Proper Means of Exterminating Insects." Anyone who examines this type of literature, however, will be forced to acknowledge that its authors when challenged to reconcile what were on their face apparently extreme contradictions, would rarely be at a loss for ingenious solutions adequate to satisfy a vast reading public determined to accept the doctrine of a wise, omnipotent, and benevolent providence.

As I shall have occasion in a subsequent lecture to argue, optimistic providentialism played a major role in the fashioning of the social thought of the eighteenth century. The theological foundations of the doctrine, however, were mainly such as to lead to a static instead of a dynamic or an evolutionary theory of the nature of the universe. This applied also to the "scientific" evidence in support of optimistic providentialism accumulated in the seventeenth and eighteenth centuries. The special association, in the minds of modern scholars, of eighteenth-century thought with the idea of progress can be supported only by concentrating on writers of the period who either failed to construct a harmonious system or were a minority of outsiders, heretics of one species or another, who accepted little of the prevailing providential doctrine of the period except the one proposition that the order and regularity perceivable in the universe could be explained only as the product of design by an intelligent being.

I should point out that, while there is no difficulty in discovering instances in the scientific literature of the period of what now seems extraordinarily naive credulity in finding providential fitnesses of natural phenomena to human needs, some modern accounts of the extent of such naiveté should be treated with caution. It was the practice of some anonymous wits of the period, especially in France, to invent fantastic examples of such fitnesses and attribute them falsely to particular providentialists. I am doubtful, for instance, that there can be traced back to a genuine text of a scientific adherent of providentialism any of the following examples which have been widely used to indicate the absurd lengths to which the doctrine was then carried by men of stature: that the variety of shades of green in the landscape had been designed to rest the eyes of observers; that the seacoasts had been so arranged as to facilitate the entrance of ships into ports; that great rivers had been so located as to pass by and thus serve the great cities that were in time to arise; that the melon had been given many sides so as to facilitate its being eaten *en famille*. It is safe,

I think, to take these examples as the fabrications of irreverent cynics who had no pious scruples as to where to seek their fun.

Finally, I must now say something to support my belief that the optimistic providentialism of the seventeenth and eighteenth centuries was not shared by those in the Augustinian tradition whether Protestant or Catholic. For them the doctrines of the Fall of Man, the curse of Adam, the second Fall of Man and the Flood, were insurmountable barriers to acceptance of optimistic pictures of the destiny of man while on this earth. I know of no evidence that any of the strict Augustinians in English or Scottish or Dutch or Genevese Calvinism, or any of the Jansenists, participated in the search for evidences of the activity of a benevolent providence in the physical nature of the earth. Their stress was on the majesty, the omnipotence, the sovereignty of God, not on his benevolence to man while he lived in sin on this earth.

There is recent literature of some dimensions purporting to show that there was a special affinity, at least in England, between Calvinism, or Puritanism, and science in the second half of the seventeenth century and later. What skepticism I have found as to the validity of this thesis turns chiefly on whether scientific achievement was exclusively Protestant or Calvinist. I would concede that if any educated Englishman in the seventeenth century was austere and sober in his mode of life, believed that salvation was to be sought through activity serviceable to mankind on this earth rather than by monastic contemplation or performance of ecclesiastical ceremonies, he was more likely to engage in the disciplined toils of scientific inquiry than if he were a Cavalier rake or roisterer. That is about all I am willing to concede after some investigation of both primary and secondary sources. Instead, however, of finding a multitude of instances of scientists who were authentic believers in the full rigor of the Augustinian doctrine of original sin, the only instances I have found to date in England, in Scotland, in Holland, in Geneva, or among the Jansenists, were Pascal in France and in England possibly Wallis and Graunt, who were by repute "Calvinists," but about whose theological views I have failed to find substantial information. It can be shown that many of the original members of the Royal Society who have been cited as examples of the special affinity between Calvinism and science had no institutional or family associations with orthodox Calvinism and that some of those who did unquestionably have a Calvinist background or ancestry were at least by 1660 rebels against Calvinist orthodoxy, and were in later terminology "moderates" if on the criteria of orthodoxy they were not even worse. At the least, the evidence is overwhelming that optimistic providentialism had its roots in the Enlightenment, and in the "secularization" of even religious thought, more than in traditional Christian orthodoxy when that is understood in the Augustinian sense. In fact, I think I have some evidence for the thesis that in England, in Scotland, and in Geneva scientific interest and achievement were associated with "lapsed Calvinism," and with rebellion against Calvinism, instead of with adherence to orthodox Calvinist theology.

I have in this lecture said virtually nothing specific about what is supposed to be the topic of these lectures, the role of providence in the social order. It seemed to me necessary, however, to sketch the historical background of providentialist thought in general before I could venture with any chance of success to make clear the religious and the intellectual foundations of seventeenth- and eighteenth-century social providentialism.

II. The Providential Elements in the Commerce of Nations

IN THIS LECTURE I deal with the history of two providentialist ideas relating to the economic status of man living in society which have played roles in the evolution of economic thought although mostly without having caught the notice of historians of that evolution. These ideas have ancient origins.

The earliest in time of these two ideas expounds a providential relative abundance of necessaries as compared with luxuries. Plato, early in the fourth century, B.C., stated that only what is rare commands a high price and that water, which is the best of all things, is also the cheapest. He offered no explanation, however, and did not expressly attribute the fact, if such it is, to providential design. Epicurus, several decades later, was in effect to repeat this proposition, and add to it an express attribution of the phenomenon to providence. "Gratitude," he wrote, "is due to blessed nature because she has made life's necessities easy of acquisition and those things difficult of acquisition unnecessary."

Pufendorf, in about the 1670's, discovered the idea in a book by Vitruvius, a Roman architect of the first century B.C., and embraced it with some enthusiasm. It is probable that it was through Pufendorf that eighteenth-century writers became acquainted with the idea. In his *De Architectura,* Vitruvius, as reported by Pufendorf, after citing water as an example of things essential to the maintenance of human life which exist in abundance, proceeded as follows:

> The divine mind has not made those things which are specially necessary to mankind as inaccessible and expensive as are pearls, gold, silver, and the like, which neither our body nor our nature

requires, but has poured forth ready to hand throughout all the world what is necessary for the safety of our mortal life.

I have not found the idea expressed or implied in the Old Testament. It thus seems to have had a pagan origin. The first statement of it in the Christian era that I have found is by Clement of Alexandria (150?-220 A.D.) in his *Paidagogos* (The Teacher): "God supplies us, first of all, with the necessities such as water and the open air, but other things that are not necessary [such as gold and pearls] He has hidden in the earth and sea." I have found a fair number of statements of this idea thereafter, continuing into at least the middle of the eighteenth century. Among the writers who expounded it, in addition to Pufendorf, were Moise Amyraut, John Locke, Daniel Defoe, Christian von Wolff. The last in time of the statements of it that I have encountered were by Francis Hutcheson, Adam Smith's teacher at Glasgow, who was steeped in Pufendorf's writings. One of Hutcheson's statements of the idea runs as follows: "By the wisdom and goodness of Providence really important things are more abundant and cheaper than those which a wise man would regard of little use."

No writer developed the idea with any degree of elaboration. Amyraut, a Huguenot of Arminian, that is, in my terminology, of optimistic, tendencies, recognized that even so-called "necessaries" might have substitutes, and carried the idea of providential abundance a step further by claiming that where what was ordinarily an essential commodity or natural circumstance was lacking, providence would have seen to it that a favorable offsetting circumstance would exist nearby to make up for the deficiency. Where the weather is cold, forests to supply wood for fuel are likely to abound. Where wood is lacking, there will be available either burnable earth (he had turf in mind, I presume) or burnable stones (coal, I presume, is meant). Where the supply of water for beasts of burden is scarce, there will be suitable animals available (camels, I suppose) which can go without water for several days. Where the soil is not suitable for growing wheat it provides roots which men can use for food.

Charles Rollin, an eighteenth-century professor of literature at the Collège de France, whose writings my learned colleague at Princeton, Professor Samuel Howell, tells me were well known in England and influenced the teaching of criticism in the English and Scottish universities, included, in the eighteenth-century pattern, some optimistic theologizing in his teaching of his special discipline. As one instance, he pointed out that sea fish of species useless to man stay in waters remote from places of human habitation, while the most edible kinds of sea fish are guided by the hand of providence even to enter the mouths of rivers and to run up them to their sources so as to bring the advantages of the sea to such peoples as live at a distance from it.

In my first lecture, I ventured the generalization that it was mainly the followers of what I have labeled as the optimistic strain in theology who sought evidence in nature of the benevolence of providence with respect to man's life on this earth, and that those who emphasized the adverse effects of the Fall on the temporal life of man either paid no attention to such doctrine or rejected it as heretical. I find confirmation of this generalization in the history of the idea of the providential abundance of necessaries as compared to the scarcity of luxuries. Except for an isolated "Pensée" of Pascal of doubtful relevance, I have found the idea only in the writings of men who clearly belong in the optimistic strain of theological thinking with respect to man's status in his earthy life.

A seventeenth-century English scientist, John Woodward, who still finds occasional mention in histories of science for both his genuine scientific discoveries and his fantastic scientific errors, strove to find in geological and botanical facts evidences of the historical validity of the account in Genesis of the adverse physical consequences for man of his fall. He used as his text the verses in Genesis 3: 17-19: "cursed is the ground for thy sake; in toil shall thou eat of it all the days of thy life; thorns also and thistles shall it bring forth to thee; and thou shalt eat the herb of the field; in the sweat of thy face shalt thou eat bread, till thou return unto the ground." Woodward, taking what he could see of the relative state of prosperity of thistles and wheat in his own time as data for the purpose of verification of Genesis, found not only that thistles were thriving, but that they were in their character apparently "more mischievous, troublesome, and molesting" to man than they once had been, although he conceded that he had not as yet found geological evidence as to what their character had been before the Fall of Man. As for wheat, he attributed to post-Fall developments the severity of the contemporary obstacles to its successful cultivation in the shape of impoverished soil, poor seed, and adverse climatic conditions. These changes favorable to thistles and unfavorable to wheat he attributed to God's decision to make the earth better suited for the moral disciplining which man needed in his lapsed state. This belief in the abundance of nuisance conditions and the scarcity of conditions favorable to the temporal life of man was of course an exact opposite to the idea of a contrast between the providential abundance of things important for man's temporal life and the scarcity of unimportant things. It is a reasonable surmise that had later expounders of the idea of the providential abundance of necessaries known of John Woodward's contradictory thesis and thought it was being widely accepted, they would have sought for evidence that thistles were in fact scarce, or were at least only a minor pest, or were in some subtle way really a blessing.

Economists interested in the history of their own discipline should not brush aside the idea of the providential abundance of necessaries as merely pious folklore involving a type of mishandling of economic phenomena from which training in economics would have provided effective protection. It is true that the idea probably involves a perverse transposing of causes and effects such as is common in providentialist thought, as, for instance by explaining the scarcity of particular commodities by their "luxury" status, instead of *vice versa.* But John Locke and Francis Hutcheson, and, except for the absence in this particular instance of express recognition of a providential role, Adam Smith himself, a trio of no mean standing in the history of economics, were among the expounders of the idea of the abundance of necessaries. It is true also that almost by definition commodities properly regarded as "necessaries" had to be abundant and cheap if men were also to be abundant and destined to survive. But economists found it a tough problem to resolve the so-called "diamond-water paradox," that is, the apparently inverse correlation between market values of particular commodities and their use-values, or religious values, or ethical or aesthetic values, or functional or technological values. There are still economists who believe that such resolution awaited the new light brought by the marginal utility analysis of the Austrian School in the 1870's. There may even today be economists who do not have full assurance that it has yet been satisfactorily resolved. But the "diamond-water paradox" is but another term for the impression of strangeness and of indication of a questionable state of human morality which St. Augustine, and a long line of succeeding theologians probably extending to the present day, drew from the low value in the market of living creatures like mice, or horses, as compared to pearls, or of water as compared to diamonds. There is a once standard, and perhaps still standard, doctrine in moral philosophy, stemming from Aristotle, of the "scale of values." This doctrine ranks the values of things according to their kinds without reference to quantities. Its expounders, I think, would have been helpless in dealing with the diamond-water paradox if some unkind person had brought it to their attention.

The field of general value theory offers perhaps the best available illustration of the general proposition that when two disciplines are at all interrelated in subject matter and share somewhat promiscuously a common vocabulary without having uniform meanings for its terms, each discipline will inevitably lose something in intelligibility to members of the other discipline and is liable also to lose some of its own coherence. The most obvious danger is that members of the different disciplines will be persuaded that they are saying the same things because their statements have similar sounds whereas these statements may have nothing in common except vocabulary and may even be in sharp if invisible conflict with each other. As long, however, as each such discipline fails to adopt or is prevented from adopting a unique jargon for itself, there will not be any remedy for this difficulty except extra care on the part of the scholar to attain precision of definition and to avoid ambiguity.

The second idea whose history I will trace in this lecture is somewhat complicated and can perhaps be most clearly formulated by presenting it as consisting of the combination of two sub-ideas: (1) providence favors trade between peoples as a means of promoting the universal brotherhood of man; (2) to give economic incentives to peoples to trade with each other providence has given to their respective territories different products. The first full statement of these propositions in combination was, as far as is known, made in the fourth century A.D. It emerged, however, from a complex set of historical and intellectual antecedents, which I will try to sketch before giving an account of the later fortunes of the doctrine.

In ancient times in the eastern Mediterranean region transport by water was much more feasible and much less expensive than overland transport because of the difficulties of the terrain and the absence of good roads, as well as because of the normal advantages of water transport over land transport at all times and in all places where the two are practically available alternatives. In that region, water transport meant as a rule sea transport, since navigable rivers were few and usually not located conveniently to densely populated regions. Interregional commerce and overseas commerce were therefore substantially synonymous. There was prevalent throughout the area an ambivalent set of attitudes towards the sea and another ambivalent set of attitudes towards commerce, reflecting religious, ethical, aesthetic, and political considerations, as well as more strictly economic ones. In principle, attitudes towards commerce and attitudes towards the sea could be at opposite poles; in practice the association between the sea and commerce was so close that it was difficult to be simultaneously enthusiastic for commerce and a hater of the sea, or a lover of the sea and a despiser of commerce. This held true in pre-Christian times for both Greek and Roman intellectuals, and I think I could show that it was also true for the writers of the Old Testament.

The attitudes towards the sea and towards commerce were determined only in part by strictly economic considerations, but these were treated as important. Economic arguments in favor of the sea, aside from its providing a source of fish, were largely confined to its serviceability as a channel for transportation of goods for commercial purposes. Economic arguments for commerce were that it provided a means of mutual exchange of goods in surplus, or mutual provision of goods in short supply, and that it gave remunerative employment to sailors and merchants.

The objections to commerce on economic grounds sometimes rested on an outright denial that interregional commerce and even local commerce conferred any net economic benefits as compared to the self-sufficiency of regions or even of private estates. More usually, however, the objectors on economic grounds to commerce specified particular drawbacks. Commerce, it was claimed, generated temptations to cheating and to exploitation where the innocent and the unsophisticated would be the victims. Overseas commerce led to dependence for essential goods on distant sources of supply, which could be costly in times of war or other emergency. Foreign commerce tended to foster tastes for exotic commodities and for luxuries, and the import of luxuries tended to impoverish a country. Overseas commerce involved great hazards to sailors, to ships, and to cargoes, from shipwreck and other casualties of the sea.

The objections raised against commerce on non-economic grounds were many. It was held to be degrading for the persons directly participating in it, to foster avarice, to bring undesirable contact with foreign persons, customs, manners, and ideas, and thus to corrupt the native culture, to give rise to strategic risks, and to breed wars. Objections were also made to commerce on religious grounds. Contact with other countries led to the intrusion into the country of the cults of foreign gods. Commerce by ships was in itself an impious activity, since braving the winds and the seas and the construction of large vessels was an affront to providence, which intended the seas to be barriers to the contact of peoples instead of a means of bringing them into communication with each other.

Especially objectionable to some, as flagrant encroachments on providence, were projects to build canals in order to promote commerce. Herodotus relates that when the Cnidians were digging a trench across an isthmus near Rhodes to make an island of their peninsula many of the diggers suffered injuries, and the project made slow progress. To envoys sent to Delphi to find out what was wrong, the priestess at Delphi warned that the digging should stop; if Zeus had wished the Cnidian land to be an island he would have long ago made it so. Pliny the elder, in his *Natural History,* relates that successive attempts of Demetrius, Caesar, Caligula, and Nero to build a ship canal across the Peloponnesian peninsula to join the Aegean and Ionian seas had all ended in failure. To Pliny this was proof that to build such a canal was an act of sacrilege. The canal was in fact finally completed—in 1893!

Most modern commentators seem to find that the preponderant attitude of the pagan Greeks and Romans towards commerce was hostile. It seems, however, that as far as Rome was concerned there has been undue reliance on the texts of a few poets who were expressing personal views often reflecting individual idiosyncracies or situations and out of rapport with the prevailing opinion of the time. I have often run across, in writings from the eighteenth century to the present day, generalizations as to the hostility of the Romans to commerce, where the sole or principal evidence specifically cited to support the generalization is a verse in one of Horace's odes in which he asserts: "in vain has God in his providence parted land from land by the estranging ocean (*Oceanus disassociabilis*), if nevertheless impious barks bound across the waters that should not be touched." I have read, however, that Horace's personality, including his susceptibility to seasickness as well as his aesthetic allergy to the sea, points, in fact, to his utter unreliability as a reporter of Roman attitudes in general towards the sea and commerce. Poets have often been acute and penetrating critics of their age, but that is not quite the same as being a reliable reporter of its prevailing opinions, which alone is relevant here. Similarly another Roman poet, Propertius, occasionally is used by modern commentators for documentation to show that, at what incidentally happened to be the height of Roman commercial enterprise and naval adventure, the Romans generally abominated the sea and despised commerce. Propertius, I am told, was an uplander, with an agrarian bias, and, like Horace, susceptible to seasickness. Basically he disliked the sea, the seashore, cities, and the bustle of trade. He had a lady-love, however, who enjoyed sea travel, liked to play on the beach at the seaside resorts of the time, and loved to swim. So Propertius blew hot and cold about the sea, speaking with some warmth of its charms when Cynthia was being kind and venting hostile reflections about the sea, apt for quotation by modern commentators, when Cynthia was being cold to him. There is much to be said for the effusions of poets. As primary sources for the historian, however, they are, like all other kinds of effusions, I suppose, to be treated with caution and discrimination.

In any case, there is an abundance of Greek and Latin source material, some of it written by poets, which expresses admiration of the sea and treats commerce as a respectable and even honorable activity. It was not, however, until the fourth century A.D. that the first explicit formulation I know of the idea of a favorable interest of providence in international trade was written. The author was Libanius, a teacher in Antioch; the work in which it appeared, when translated from its Greek original, was given the title, *Orationes;* the formulation was as follows:

> God did not bestow all products upon all parts of the earth, but distributed His gifts over different regions, to the end that men might cultivate a social relationship because one would have need of the help of another. And so he called commerce into being, that

all men might be able to have common enjoyment of the fruits of earth, no matter where produced.

Libanius was a pagan, but among his students were two young men who were destined to be Church Fathers, St. Basil and St. John Chrysostom. Both directly and through these Fathers of the Church the idea was to enter what for the purposes of these lectures I call the optimistic strain in Christian theology. The emphasis on the universal brotherhood of man reveals a late Stoic influence on Libanius's thought. On the other hand, a modern scholar has interpreted Libanius's emphasis throughout his writings on the providential concern for the temporal welfare of mankind as showing his desire to strengthen the old pagan religion's ability to withstand the rising competition of Christianity by borrowing from the latter its humanitarian warmth and its sensitivity to human needs and aspirations. This seems plausible to me. If it is correct, then Libanius is to be interpreted both as influenced by Christianity and as having through his writings and his students contributed to Christian theology an idea which was later to be accepted by many Christians as one of that theology's most admirable elements, namely, the idea that God intended commerce to operate as a unifying factor for all mankind.

I have found in the writings of four early Christian theologians statements of the doctrine of the providential function of commerce, all following closely Libanius's formulation. Of these four, two are St. Basil and St. John Chrysostom, who, as I have said, were students of Libanius at Antioch, a third is Theodoretus, Bishop of Cyrus and a theologian of the school of Antioch, and the fourth is St. Ambrose, whose *Hexameron* (or the Six Days) was a free adaptation in Latin of St. Basil's work of the same title written in Greek. It is of course highly probable that thorough search of the writings of the Fathers of the church by a qualified scholar would disclose additional formulations of the idea. On the evidence I have found, however, it seems to me practically certain that at least one way by which the idea entered into the Christian tradition was via Libanius both directly and through his Christian students. The comments on commerce of other Fathers are, as far as I know, never as favorable as is the Libanius doctrine. Many of them are in fact distinctly hostile, partly on the basis of the association of trade of any kind with fraud and exploitation, partly because of the association of trade with avarice and luxury, and partly because of lack of recognition of or indifference to its potential material benefits to mankind.

I have found in secondary sources citations of a moderate number of explicit statements of the providential interest in commerce from theological treatises of the high Middle Ages, several of them by influential and otherwise important writers, for instance, Henri de Langenstein in the fourteenth century, St. Antoninus of Florence in the fifteenth century, Giovanni Botero in the early sixteenth century. These all correspond more or less closely to Libanius's formulation, which had already apparently become somewhat of a standard one. It was common at least by the fourteenth century for international fairs to be blessed by priests at their opening. In one such fourteenth-century instance the presiding cleric used a formula which, translated from the Latin, runs as follows:

> God has wished that no country should be able to be completely self-sufficing by itself, and that each country should have need of seeking supplies from other countries, in order that they should all become united by friendly ties.

The modern writer who reports this, adds the comment: "one can see that the thought which presides over our present-day international fairs is not of yesterday." He apparently was not aware that it stemmed, without significant change, from Libanius in the fourth century A.D. In modern times, when the idea that international trade is highly beneficial to mankind has been widely and even enthusiastically accepted, sympathetic students of the economic writings of the scholastics have occasionally claimed to have found the idea that such trade has a providential blessing quite widespread among them. I am somewhat skeptical of this, as they all seem to give very much the same limited set of references to the scholastic literature, while they tend to neglect the abundance of instances where scholastics repeat the old objections to foreign trade on religious and moral grounds.

It would be interesting to know, in this connection, just where St. Thomas Aquinas stood. One modern authority on scholastic economics has referred to a passage in St. Thomas's works which apparently in effect echoes Libanius's formulation. Elsewhere in his writings, however, St. Thomas follows faithfully enough the old objections to foreign trade on the grounds of the economic merits of self-sufficiency, the threat to internal political peace which results from the presence of many foreigners, the liability to corruption of morals and manners which much contact with foreigners entails, and so forth. He introduces, moreover, what seems to me a novel note in the treatment of this topic; he invokes the Aristotelian "scale of values" doctrine to support the merit of economic self-sufficiency:

> . . . the higher a thing is the more self-sufficient it is; since whatever needs another's help is by that fact proven inferior.
>
> A city which has an abundance of food from its own territory is more dignified than one which is provisioned by merchants.

St. Thomas does not insist, however, at this point or elsewhere, on complete autarchy even as an ideal. There are few instances, he says, where a city can provide all its necessaries by its own productive services, and if a city has surpluses of some commodities, loss to many of the citizens would result if it was not permitted to professional merchants to export such surpluses abroad. "Consequently," said St. Thomas, "[even] the perfect city will make a moderate use of merchants."

By the end of the sixteenth century the idea was appearing with some frequency in lay literature both in Protestant and in Catholic countries. In the seventeenth and eighteenth centuries it had become a commonplace, a familiar maxim, but increasingly it was being converted from a merely fashionable or edifying formula to a functional idea, an argument by which to influence national policy. To the limited extent to which it continued to remain in circulation in the nineteenth century, this use provided the main excuse for stating it. The most recent statement of the idea in England that I have found, however, was in 1887, in an almost purely theological treatise.

In the United States, the latest exposition of the idea that I have encountered was by a Congressman from Missouri in the House of Representatives in 1894 speaking in support of the low-tariff Wilson Tariff Bill. The relevant passage is somewhat long, but I will quote it nevertheless because to my ear the first half is Libanius translated into Congressional rhetoric and the second half is Adam Smith expounded in even purer Americanese:

> God could have made this world, if He had wanted to, with exactly the same climate and soil all over it, so that each nation would have been entirely independent of any other nation. But He didn't do that. He made this world so that every nation in it has got to depend for something upon some other nations. He did that to promote kinship among the different people. Let us drop this unnatural business. There is no end to the ingenuity of man. You can fix up a scheme, if you want, for raising oranges in Maine, but a barrel of those oranges would make William Waldorf Astor's pocketbook sick. . . . You can raise polar bears on the Equator if you spend money enough, but it would take a king's ransom to do it.

The illustration used by Adam Smith to make the same point was raising grapes in Scotland:

> By means of glasses, hotbeds, and hotwalls, very good grapes can be raised in Scotland . . . but at about thirty times the expence for which at least equally good can be brought from foreign countries.

I have not made an extensive search for additional formulations of the idea by American writers, and I know of only a handful. One of these I will have occasion to quote later. Another one I will quote at once, as it comes from a founding member of the Society that is sponsoring these lectures. In 1729, in his first work dealing with economic matters, Benjamin Franklin wrote:

> As Providence has so ordered it, that not only different countries, but even different parts of the same country, have their peculiar most suitable productions, and likewise that different men have geniuses adapted to variety of different arts and manufactures, therefore commerce, or the exchange of one commodity or manufacture for another, is highly convenient and beneficial to mankind.

As compared with Libanius's formula, this omits mention of the promotion of fraternity between peoples as the objective of providence. But from the economist's point of view it has the merit of adding differences in the skills of different peoples as a factor in making commerce beneficial.

I have the impression that there are few ideas of comparable age, subtlety, and prevalence with the idea whose history I have been commenting on, which have so often been expressed with no indication of awareness of their past, and which have so often been received by modern scholars who encounter them in a text as being both important and novel. The origin of the idea of the interest of providence in commerce has been attributed by scholars to Bodin, to Calvin, to an English scholastic of the fourteenth century, Richard of Middleton, to an Italian Renaissance writer, L. B. Alberti, to Grotius, and to any number of others. In April, 1914, a French Catholic priest, in a contribution to a religious periodical, stated the idea, in the form of a prayer, with no significant departure from or addition to Libanius's formula, as part of a plea, a very timely plea, for friendly relations between countries. This constitutes the very latest statement of the idea not presented explicitly as a quotation from an earlier writer which I have encountered anywhere. This statement was quoted in 1932 at the annual congress of an important French Catholic organization specializing in social ethics where it was characterized as "a beautiful prayer" of "profoundly Catholic inspiration." I suspect that both speaker and audience at the 1932 meeting were totally unaware that the idea had been in fairly constant circulation in substantially the same formulation for at least 1,500 years.

I have already pointed out that in the sixteenth to eighteenth centuries the idea was frequently used in a functional way, that is, to influence national economic policy. This was the age of mercantilism, and, given my biases, I find it hard to think of any idea whose acceptance as a ruling idea by those then in power would under the circumstances of the time have had a greater potential for benefit to mankind. We can be sure that no one who then expounded it was using it to support objectives equivalent to what we now call free trade. In France and in England it was being used domestically to support the liberalization or moderation of existing restrictions on foreign trade. By the Protestant jurists like Grotius, Pufendorf, and Vattel, it was used against outright prohibitions of trade and against national monopolies of fisheries and trade routes. I am unable to judge whether the idea then had any material consequences, but it may at least have troubled the consciences of those who were as rulers and legislators extending and intensifying restrictions on trade.

In late sixteenth- and seventeenth-century France, there was much internal complaint against the severity of the mercantilist restrictions on foreign trade which were then in force. The objectors had in mind not only the effects of the restrictions on themselves and on the French economy, but also the almost continuous warfare with which the restrictions were associated and for which they may have been in part responsible. Time and again these objectors used as a religious and moral argument against existing policy the doctrine of the providential interest in commerce as generating friendly relations between peoples. They succeeded at times in putting the government on the defensive and in forcing it to reformulate the case for its policies and practices in less aggressive and less amoral terms. This was not a contest, I repeat, between free trade and mercantilism, for practically everyone with ideas about national economic policy was then a mercantilist, but between moderate and extreme mercantilism. At the least, it forced the government to restate its objectives in terms which were less obviously in conflict with some widely accepted religious and ethical views.

In France, however, and to some degree in England also, ingenious polemicists succeeded somewhat in turning the flank of those who used the providentialist argument by giving it a twist which enabled the most extreme mercantilists to adopt it as their own. French extremist mercantilists took to saying that since it was providence which had chosen France as the sole country which had sufficient range and extent of resources to do without any imports of necessaries; severe restraints on importation, no matter how far they went, could not therefore for her be action in violation of providential intent.

Belief in complete or nearly complete self-sufficiency as a practicable and desirable national objective was peculiar to France. In England the doctrine of a providential interest in commerce was twisted to serve extreme mercantilist programs by applying it to particular commodities or trades. Providence had assigned to England the production of certain commodities or the monopoly of certain particular trades. It was therefore following the guidance of providence, not opposing it, to promote these industries or trades. Also, when providence assigned to England the production of a particular raw material, like wool, it must also have assigned to England its processing into woolens. This reasoning was extended to the acquisition of colonies. Providence had staked out for English acquisition and settlement certain overseas areas of the world; the rival claims of other imperialist countries or of the native inhabitants therefore had no standing.

As an illustration of the application of this type of reasoning to the wool-woolens issue I cite from Martin Bucer, one of the leading Protestant reformers, who in 1549 to 1551 was in England as a professor of theology at Cambridge University, an adviser of government, and an expounder of the new Reformed religion. England, he advised, should process its own wool:

> For one should not express doubt that the Lord who had so abundantly endowed the English with wool had not also wished that they should employ themselves in the working-up of the wool into cloth and applying it to the uses of this human life, and not to transport it abroad to be processed there, while they themselves lived in idleness.

How do such writers discover in advance, when the interests of rival nations conflict, which nation providence will choose to prefer, and how is it that they almost invariably find that it is their own nation? I suppose the answer is that pious patriotism is a natural product of the psychological propensity to find affinity between cherished ideas. John Milton, in the course of an exposition of progressive revelation, claims that England is usually the first beneficiary of new revelation:

God is decreeing to begin some new and great period in his Church, even to the reforming of Reformation itself: what then does He do but reveal Himself to his servants, and as his manner is, first to his Englishmen; I say as His manner is, first to us, though we mark not the method of his counsels, and are unworthy.

Charles Dickens, in his characterization in *Our Mutual Friend,* of the London merchant, Mr. Podsnap, pictures him as complacent both about England, which is to him in no respect "unworthy," and about the superiority of his own personal qualities:

"Mr. Podsnap was sensible of its being required of him to take Providence under his protection. . . . And it was very remarkable (and must have been very comfortable) that what Providence meant, was invariably what Mr. Podsnap meant." Dickens has Mr. Podsnap say that in its constitution England was favored by providence over all other countries. When the Frenchman with whom he was conversing was on the point of asking how it happened that providence selected England for favors above all other countries, Podsnap interrupted him to say: "This island was blest, sir, to the direct exclusion of such other countries as . . . there may happen to be."

There was little direct criticism of the idea of a providential interest in commerce by either clerics or laymen. Exponents of it in general put no heavy reliance on Biblical texts to support it, in part, no doubt, because they are not easy to find. The idea was treated by its supporters substantially as an element in natural rather than in revealed theology, and searchers of the Scriptures found in them more hostility to than welcoming of commerce. Luther, for example, claimed that God did not like commerce and let his people of Israel live by the sea and yet not engage in commerce. It was much more godly, said Luther, "to till the land than to engage in commerce, and those do better who follow the Scriptures in exploiting the soil and seeking their nourishment from it." A modern Lutheran theologian, Karl Holl, explains this attitude of Luther as a reaction to the moral teaching of the scholastics who, he says, at all points preferred the city dweller to the peasant.

Lay writers sometimes expounded doctrine inconsistent with the usual version of the providential interest in commerce. Daniel Defoe, early in the eighteenth century, while insisting that "there is a kind of divinity in the origin of trade" found this divine origin of trade not, or perhaps not only, in a providential desire to promote universal brotherhood, but in the regional dispersion of natural resources designed by providence to force mankind to get its subsistence by hard work. If all the productions of the world should have been found in every part, getting commodities would have been too easy.

> But wise providence having resolved man to eat his bread with the sweat of his brow, . . . has, to this purpose, placed the several blessings he has bestowed on the world for the use and convenience of man, at the remotest distance from one another, in the most secret, reserv'd and inaccessible parts, and shared to all parts of the earth something essential to the other, so as to make a universal correspondence absolutely necessary.

Defoe, however, explains that he is not here rejecting what I earlier in this lecture called the idea of the providential abundance of necessaries:

> It is true, the common mercies of life, and such as mankind can least want [i.e., do without] our bountiful creator has made most universal; such as water for drink, corn and cattle for food.

Voltaire, on the other hand, less disposed than Defoe to find his guidance in the Scriptures, could see only mystery in the pattern of world distribution of the earth's fruits: providence ripens in Mocha, in the hot sands of Arabia, the coffee so necessary for the countries of frost; it puts the fever in our climates, and the remedy in America. The authors (W. and R. Chambers) of an elementary textbook in economics, published in Edinburgh in 1852, who included in it a statement in very much its standard form of the idea of a providential interest in commerce, replied to Voltaire's objection by appealing to the promotion of international good will which commerce involves. "If we ever see a time when war shall cease, it will be when nations are so dependent on each other for the necessaries and comforts of life that they cannot afford to quarrel."

Adam Smith has puzzled many commentators by his attribution of the origin of commerce to a subrational propensity to truck and barter, rather than to a rational pursuit of economic benefit. An Anglican clergyman, Richard Raikes, in 1806, in an elaborate exposition of the providential interest in commerce, makes use of Adam Smith's notion of an instinct to barter. Smith never explicitly formulates the idea that providence favors commerce, but it is implicit in his writings; and I am not at all sure that Raikes has not hit upon the most satisfactory explanation available of why Smith explained the initial resort of men to trade by a psychological propensity instead of by the usual appeal to a rational or utilitarian search for gain.

I should mention also the questioning in *Crito*, 1766, by its idiosyncratic author, James Burgh, of the common belief that the abundance of seas was intended to promote commerce, on the ground that

> that end would have been better answered by a multitude of navigable rivers at convenient distances from one another, as in the American and other continents, than by covering the greatest part of the surface of the globe with immense oceans, whose frightful vastness and mountainous rolling so discouraged navigators unfurnished with the compass and unskilled in their art, that almost five thousand years elapsed [from the time of the

Flood] before one half of the globe came to be known to the inhabitants of the other.

There is in Genesis a text which has been an obstacle to acceptance on religious grounds of a universalistic or cosmopolitan approach to international relations. This is the account of the "confusion of tongues" brought about by Jehovah as a reproof to the people from many lands who assembled at Babel to build a tower "whose top may reach unto heaven, and let us make us a name; lest we be scattered abroad upon the face of the whole earth." I have failed to find a historical account of the interpretation of the Genesis story by believers through the ages, and can do no more here than to report several interesting comments on the tower of Babel story that I have run across, which provide a contrast to the history of the idea of a favorable interest of providence in close economic and other relations between peoples.

Philo of Alexandria, in the first century A.D. (or perhaps somewhat earlier) reports objections which scoffers had already raised against the Genesis account. The story related in Genesis, they claimed, was merely a variant of an old fable told of animals which once were able to communicate with each other in a common language but had this capacity taken away from them because they had misbehaved and because multiplication of languages would be an obstacle to their cooperating again in sinful activity. Philo left the defense of the account to literalist interpreters of the Scriptures, and he confined his own treatment of the story to a freely allegorical interpretation of it which has no relevance for my immediate theme.

A Scottish Calvinist theologian, Robert Fleming, writing in the second half of the seventeenth century, pointed out that rational men would not themselves have chosen a diversity of languages, since this would divide mankind, would be a barrier to commerce, and would obstruct the growth of human knowledge and the spread of new scientific inventions; the confusion of tongues, therefore, must have been an act of providence, instead of an act of human volition. Fleming suggests that God's purpose must have been to separate the Israelites from the rest of the world. Bishop Bossuet at about the same time used the story as a religious support for the legitimacy of national patriotism, as against cosmopolitanist doctrines. Edmund Law, an Anglican clergyman of the eighteenth century, interpreted the purpose of the diversification of languages to be a barrier to the corruption of religion by external influences. I have the impression that this last has been the most common interpretation of the story.

Goldwin Smith, in 1860, when he was professor of modern history in Oxford, interpreted the intent of providence in dividing mankind into separate nations as, in effect, to create safety-bulkheads in the form of national boundaries in the world as security against a universal corruption.

> If all mankind were one state, with one set of customs, one literature, one code of laws, and this state became corrupted, what remedy, what redemption would there be? None, but a convulsion which would rend the frame of society to pieces, and deeply injure the moral life which society is designed to guard. Not only so, but the very idea of political improvement might be lost, and all the world might become more dead than China. Nations redeem each other. They preserve for each other principles, truths, hopes, aspirations, which, committed to the keeping of one nation only, might, as frailty and error are conditions of man's being, become extinct forever.

I am tempted to assert a contrast between two rival theological traditions within Christendom, one represented by the idea of the providential interest in commerce as a unifier of mankind, the other represented by the interpretation of the confusion of tongues story as revealing a providential interest in the division of mankind into separate nations. But I know too little of the history of the reception of the Tower of Babel story to be justified in attributing the degree of historical importance to it that this would suggest.

I have found only scattered instances in the nineteenth century and since of writers who maintain as an article of personal belief of the idea that the territorial dispersion of productive resources was the result of providential design intended to promote commerce and thus to promote the unification of mankind. Several of them I have already presented to you. Several of them were economists of note, for instance, Robert Torrens and Nassau Senior in England, von Thünen in Germany. In the victorious English campaign against the corn laws in the 1840's, the religious note was prominent. The leader of the campaign, Richard Cobden, adopted as a sort of personal slogan: "Free Trade is the International Law of God," but I have not been able to find that he ever made an explicit reference to the territorial differences in productive resources as being a connecting link between the role of providence and the beneficial economic effect of commerce. A few of the many non-conformist ministers who campaigned for free trade did use as an argument the traditional formula that providence had dispersed productive resources over the earth in such a pattern that commerce became economically beneficial and thus could perform its providential function of promoting amity between peoples. The main reasons, however, given by the non-conformist clergymen for their advocacy as clergymen of free trade were; first, that under prevailing English conditions tariff protection, as they saw it, benefited chiefly the rich landowners and imposed its burdens in the form of expensive bread chiefly on the urban poor, so that considerations of charity therefore justified effort to repeal the corn laws; second, that the freer commerce was, the more likely it was that we would attain a peaceful world. With extremely rare exceptions, Anglican clergymen did not participate in the campaign for free trade; a considerable number of them, indeed, were active on the protectionist side.

It is not, I think, over-cynical to hold that theological differences between Anglicanism and Dissent had little bearing on this alignment of the two religious bodies on opposite sides of a political issue. Dissent was predominantly urban; the Church of England predominantly rural. There were strong associations of social and economic interest between the landed gentry and the Anglican Establishment. Tithes levied on agricultural produce constituted a major source of support of the Anglican clergy: the income derived from tithes was a function of the prices of agricultural products; dissenting ministers had no share in the tithes. Subconsciously at least, all of these factors may well have had a part in leading the two groups to take opposite sides on the issue of free trade versus protection.

For economic theorists the chief point, and, I fear, perhaps the only point, of technical interest to them, in the idea of the providential promotion of commerce whose history I have been tracing in this lecture, is the part played in the idea by the notion that it is the different relative abundance of various products and of different factors of production in different regions which provides the occasion for mutually profitable trade and operates to determine the volume and make-up of international trade. This notion is the foundation-stone of current international trade theory, under the designation of the Heckscher-Ohlin theory. It was first expounded with technical rigor by Eli F. Heckscher of Stockholm in 1919, and in 1933 it was elaborated in a famous book by Bertil Ohlin, also of Stockholm. Heckscher was aware of the ancient and religious origin of the idea that it is the unequal territorial dispersion of productive resources which provides the economic basis for interregional trade. It may even be that consciously or subconsciously it was this ancient idea that gave him the stimulus to formulate it in rigorous analytical terms.

As Libanius presented the idea, he referred only to territorial differences in "products" and he did not make any distinction between absolute and relative differences. This continued to be the way in which the idea was presented for a long time in its history. From perhaps the seventeenth century on, however, the idea underwent bit-by-bit elaboration, so that relative as well as absolute differences were mentioned, differences in abundance of factors of production were mentioned as well as differences in abundance of products, climatic differences and differences in skills were recognized as significant, and, perhaps most subtle of all, territorial differences in tastes and desires, as distinguished from "needs," were noticed as relevant. No one writer took account of all these considerations, but before the nineteenth century several writers recognized simultaneously a substantial number of them. What seems to me the outstanding statement in this respect, one which I have previously tried to bring to the attention of economists, was in 1768 (or earlier) by a colonial American, Thomas Hutchinson, Governor of Massachusetts, in his *History . . . of Massachusetts-Bay.* I regret that his statement is too long to be cited here in its entirety, but I will quote what for my present purposes is the more essential portion:

> The great creator of the universe in infinite wisdom has so formed the earth that different parts of it, from the soil, climate, &c. are adapted to different produce, and he so orders and disposes the genius, temper, numbers and other circumstances relative to the inhabitants as to render some employments peculiarly proper for one country, and others for another, and by this provision a

mutual intercourse is kept up between the different parts of the globe.

It is a matter for wonder that it was more than a century and a half after this quotation before economists exploited with anything approaching full adequacy the economic insight which was embodied in this passage and, in embryonic form, in writings antedating this passage by over eighteen centuries.

I know of only one economist who has ever in his discussion of the free trade versus protection issue included in it an examination of the merits and implications of the idea of a providential allocation of particular products to particular countries. John Rae, in his *New Principles on the Subject of Political Economy* (Boston, 1834), which is in large part a critique of Adam Smith's *Wealth of Nations,* interpreted Adam Smith's attack on mercantilist restrictions on trade as an application of the idea that providence having allocated particular products to particular countries, governments should not tamper with this allocation. Rae does not in principle reject providentialist argument, but he thinks that such argument on the one hand, and argument resting on secondary causes, or what he calls "inductive studies," on the other hand, should be conducted in separate compartments. Adam Smith, however, having combined them in a single treatment, Rae says he has to follow suit. Rae was a vigorous exponent of tariff protection for selected industries, especially in young countries, but probably also in old countries where some industries had not established themselves but could do so successfully if they were aided in coping with the special difficulties of their early years.

This is, of course, the already-old argument for the protection of infant industries extended, however, to the protection against foreign competition of the national economies of "young countries." Adam Smith did not deny in principle all validity to the infant-industry argument for protection. He claimed, however, that it would probably work badly in practice because of the failings of governments whose function it would be to carry out such a policy. With this type of objection to the infant-industry argument John Rae did not deal.

I know also of no exponent of the idea of the providential assignment of particular products to particular countries who said anything about such assignment being eternal and immutable. It is a valid criticism of, say, the English classical economists that they did not make it crystal clear that it was the prospective comparative advantages in production that they looked to as guides to policy, and that the existent comparative advantages were relevant only if and as they provided the best index to what the future pattern of advantage would be. On the other hand, some economists today, especially in underdeveloped countries, offer no better guide to the national allocation of resources than either promiscuous protection, or, worst of all, allocation in reverse relationship to either the existing or the prospective pattern of comparative advantage.

I have here, however, slipped deeper into technical economic analysis than is appropriate to these lectures, and into more evaluation of ideas than is orthodox for a conscientiously neutral practitioner of the art of the history of ideas. It is well, therefore, that I should end my lecture at this point, lest I travel further on a forbidden path.

III. The Invisible Hand and Economic Man

By the latter half of the seventeenth century, in both the Roman Catholic and the Protestant countries of northern and western Europe, ethical and economic thought had undergone a large measure of "secularization" or, in what seems to be its equivalent in French common usage, of "laicization." This was to proceed further in the eighteenth century. These terms are liable to be misleading, however, each in its own way. As they have been used, they do not mean a complete breakaway of ethical and economic thought from religious ideas, nor a complete transfer of the responsibility of expounding ethical and economic doctrine from clerics to laics. They represent rather a lessening of the influence on ethical and economic thought of ecclesiastical authority and traditional church creeds, and a shifting of weight from dogma and revelation and other-worldliness to reason and sentiment and considerations of temporal welfare.

There did occur relative growth in the number of laymen as compared to clergymen who had access to the best education available. Not long before, clerics had had almost a monopoly of higher learning. The process of "secularization" or of "laicization" of ethical and economic thought, however, was occurring within as well as outside the ranks of the clergy, and in some countries seems to have been more rapid among the clergy than among the masses of the people. Clergymen were often the leading expounders of a "secularized" ethics, in the name of natural theology and of natural law in the Catholic Church, and of natural theology, moral theology, and moral philosophy in some of the Protestant countries.

Catholicism had a bridge to rationalistic or naturalistic ethics in its natural law doctrine from the beginning of

55

scholastic teaching. Except for questions of ecclesiology, of ritual and liturgy, and of Christology, Anglicanism was "comprehensive" or "Latitudinarian" and tolerated a wide range of doctrine. With the partial exception of doctrine with respect to usury, it seems to be difficult to find important socio-economic doctrines which in the eighteenth century were being expounded widely within one church and rejected or ignored within another. Orthodox Lutheranism and orthodox Calvinism did not share in the secularization process to any appreciable extent. Calvinism had had from its origins a partial bridge to humanism and to a secularized ethics in Calvin's doctrine of "common grace" as distinguished from "saving grace." "Common grace," however, while it could lead to a temporally flourishing society, as outwardly righteous as the community of "saints," orderly, peaceful, and prosperous, yielded no "merit" for purposes of salvation. By most Calvinists, moreover, the doctrine of "common grace" was soon forgotten. Even the leading Calvinist historians have rediscovered the doctrine only in very recent years. So also for the most Augustinian of the Catholics, the Jansenists. Two of their most prominent expounders of social doctrine, Pierre Nicole and Jean Domat, in the second half of the seventeenth century, expounded, in order to condemn it, an ethic sufficient to make possible an orderly and prosperous society, an ethic actually being widely observed, the ethic of the "honnête homme," attractive on the outside but allegedly rotten inside, and leading its practitioners only to future damnation. Nicole's moral essays won an extraordinarily wide circulation, and were spread by writers as far removed from Jansenism as they could be, including, for instance, John Locke in England, who translated several of them. I suspect that many readers of these essays, convinced that they had little to fear, if they led an honorable life on human standards, from a God who was benevolent and reasonable, read these essays as expositions of good social ethics instead of as a warning that there was no contribution to salvation in good works unassisted by a special saving grace.

In any case, by 1700, orthodox Calvinism, like orthodox Lutheranism, had among intellectuals largely yielded to new, essentially Arminian, doctrines as to the relationship of good works to salvation. In this respect at least the Enlightenment had by the end of the eighteenth century, if not long before, brought to much of western Europe, and incidentally to Harvard, to Yale, and to some at least of the founders of the American Philosophical Society and of the Founding Fathers of the American Republic, a substantially common social ethic, the social ethic of John Locke, of Kant and Leibnitz, of Diderot and Turgot, of Bishop Butler and the Latitudinarian bishops of the Church of England, of the Moderates in Scotland and the non-Calvinist nonconformists in England, of even bishops of the Catholic Church in France and in Germany, and of most deists, whether they were "critical deists" or not. It is with this "secularized" ethics and its applications to socio-economic issues that I will be concerned in this lecture.

In the seventeenth and eighteenth century, as I related in my previous lecture, orthodox Christianity, to defend Genesis, had to contend with new science. In Britain, it also had to contend with a new ethics, which insisted on the existence of a ruling providence, but strained every effort to explain its mode of operation through secondary causes constituted by human psychology, the moral sentiments and human reason, without appeal to revelation. Between orthodoxy and the new ethics there was no important conflict as to what the actual outcome in objective human behavior should be. The orthodox insisted, however, that without general acceptance by the public of the traditional Christian doctrine with respect to a future life in which men would be rewarded and punished for their behavior in this life, moral behavior would vanish.

All of the influential British eighteenth-century theologians and moral philosophers, whatever their philosophical or theological beliefs, were agreed that once the Restoration of 1660, or once the Glorious Revolution of 1689, had occurred, neither religion nor morality called for any substantial change in the political structure, or in the social structure of England, or of Scotland. With respect to matters of more direct economic interest also, there was widespread belief that no major changes in economic institutions, policies, or patterns of behavior were urgently called for on religious or moral grounds.

The same social and political views, however, which in Britain were a reflection of the prevailing complacency about the existing social and political order, and therefore were politically and economically conservative, an apologia for the *status quo*, were in France, whose intellectuals were deeply dissatisfied with the social and political structure of the country, progressive and even radical. In France also, the abandonment of traditional theology on the part of the "Enlightened" was more extreme than in Britain, led more to atheistic or near-atheistic views, and was associated, unlike the situation in England and Scotland, with an extreme anti-clericalism.

Ethics was the heart of eighteenth-century British moral philosophy. Almost every learned Englishman, and still more every learned Scotsman, it would seem, at some stage of his career felt impelled to publish his views on "The Origin of Evil." Whatever their special field of interest, whether the natural sciences, theology, law, literary criticism, fiction, or poetry, eighteenth-century authors sought to relate their work to its ethical foundations or implications.

Eighteenth-century ethics was, and was proclaimed as being, social ethics; it concerned itself with man's behavior in society, with his social relations to other men. In whatever senses it may be true that eighteenth-century thought was "individualistic," it was not true in the sense that any important writers of the century failed to stress obligations of the individual to his community as a central datum, whether or not the sole one, of morality. The happiness of mankind was generally accepted as at least one of the ends of good behavior.

Asceticism as moral or religious doctrine was almost nonexistent in the literature, even in the sermons, of the time, if by it is meant the renunciation, for the sake of renunciation or of salvation, of worldy enjoyment and comforts by individuals or by the community in general and not merely the surrender of "vicious" pleasures or of those whose pursuit by one individual involved injury to or deprivation of other individuals. The tradition of ascetic doctrine, and of the virtue of renunciation for its own sake, still lingered in some of the pulpits of the time. Such doctrine, however, was widely regarded as "enthusiastic," or fanatic; and "enthusiasm," in this respect as in general, was in eighteenth-century Britain almost universally frowned upon or condemned outright. It was one of the paradoxes of Mandeville's *Fable of the Bees* that, while everyone thought he found in this book a strong taint of deliberate libertinism and immoralism, it was very nearly the only work of prominence in the period in which even lip-service was given, on allegedly religious grounds, to ascetic standards of behavior for the general population.

R. H. Tawney, in his prolonged campaign to persuade us that the age of capitalism was marked by a deterioration of the social ethics of the western world as compared with the age of serfdom, remarked that eighteenth-century social philosophy "repudiated teleology and substituted the analogy of a self-regulating mechanism, moved by the weights and pulleys of economic motives, for the theory which had regarded it as an organism composed of different classes united by mutual obligations springing from their common relation to a common end."

It would have been helpful if Tawney had given references, and still better, cited texts, which support his generalization. Eighteenth-century British social philosophy was in fact soaked in teleology. I know of no British writer before Bentham who frankly renounced teleology, and of no important writers except Mandeville and David Hume —and perhaps also Thomas Hobbes— who could plausibly be interpreted on the basis of their actual writings as not honestly accepting it. There is no logical conflict between teleology and automatism if ends or design have been built into the automatic mechanism itself, as was universally affirmed. There is no logical conflict between a socially oriented teleology and individualism if the individual either has conscious social ends or by providential design serves such ends without having adopted them as his own ultimate objective. There are few traces in the British eighteenth-century literature of "organic" theories of society in the nineteenth-century romantic sense. I know of no evidence, however, that any of Bishop Butler's contemporaries thought it eccentric or uncommon for him to refuse to engage in "the speculative absurdity of considering ourselves as single and independent" instead of as members of a mutually interdependent society. The ethical discussions of the eighteenth century not only did not rest on the assumption of the non-existence of "social tissue," but concerned themselves primarily with the origin, character, and strength of the existing bonds of society. The most extreme individualism in doctrine came not from religious skeptics or from deists, but from a school of Anglican theologians, the theological utilitarians, who insisted that hope of personal rewards and fear of personal punishment in a future life were essential if society was not to disintegrate into moral anarchy.

There were a number of differing and contending schools of ethics in the period, but they all dealt with essentially the same questions: (a) What is the source or nature of moral obligation? (b) What are the objective and subjective criteria of moral behavior? (c) What are the sanctions of moral behavior, how effective are they, and how can they be made more effective? The issues between the schools were intellectually of great importance, but there was considerable overlapping in membership of the respective schools. When studies of individual writers are made, it seems almost invariably to turn out that they were eclectic if not self-contradictory or undergoing change of opinion through time.

All of the schools were highly abstract in actual method, although they sometimes imagined themselves to be fully empirical. Whatever may be the implications of their respective doctrines for social policy which we can now discover, I can find not a single clear instance where the particular school of doctrine to which an author belonged had any visible influence on his position on concrete issues of social policy. To the question, what constituted virtuous behavior in terms of actual conduct, there was considerable debate as to whether the *summun bonum* was happiness, or obedience to the command of God, or the "fitness of things." Even among those who were agreed that human happiness was the highest end, there was debate as to whether prudential conduct in serving one's own interest, or service to others in the expectation of a reward from providence in this or in a future life, or service to others out of pure benevolence or love of God or love of virtue, were all to be classified alike as "virtuous" conduct. The relative importance of intent and of actual consequences was also much debated. On the abstract level on which these latter discussions were conducted, they had no obvious significance for concrete social issues. Important as these issues may be for theology and ethics, therefore, they need not be pursued here.

The question whether human happiness was the *summun bonum,* however, could have had an important bearing on social attitudes if there had been an important and influential school which maintained that there was a higher end which involved systematic and major sacrifice of human happiness. There was advocacy of voluntary personal sacrifice in the interest of the greater happiness of others or of the community as a whole, and of the surrender or renunciation of temporal goods should they stand in the way of happiness in a future life. There was reiterated enunciation of the ancient maxim that the deliberate and calculated pursuit of personal happiness was not an efficient way of attaining it. There was considerable discussion, which nineteenth-century utilitarianism, to its loss, was to neglect, of the respective merits of adherence to good general rules and the fostering of good habits, on the one hand, and separate decisions, *ad hoc,* on the individual merits of each case as it arose, on the other hand. There was, nevertheless, an important measure of utilitarianism of some species in practically all of British eighteenth-century moral philosophy.

Most important for our present purposes were the controversies as to what constituted the sanctions for or inducements to moral behavior, and as to their comparative effectiveness. From Hobbes's time on for over a century, it was a major purpose of British moral philosophy to find a persuasive answer to Hobbes's doctrine on these points. Hobbes accepted the doctrine of a law of nature which dictated to man what it was right for him to do. Man, however, was so constituted that he did not obey the law of nature in the absence of some form of coercion. In a state of nature—that is, in the absence of civil government—man, driven by his strongest "passions," and especially the desire of safety, the desire of gain, the desire of glory, and the desire of power, would be in constant warfare with his neighbors. In the state of nature, consequently, man's life was "solitary, poor, nasty, brutish and short," was a state of "war . . . of every man, against every man." At some stage, men, seeking peace, entered into a compact between themselves to set up civil government, and endowed government with practically unlimited authority. Hobbes preferred an absolute monarchy, but he did not reject the possibility of democratic government. The law of nature, which in the state of nature was morally binding but was not obeyed, he continues to accept, in a shadowy sense, as obligatory in civil society. But the effective authority in all matters is now the sovereign. If the sovereign follows it, the law of nature now receives its first practical application. But whatever the character of the positive laws of the sovereign, with the one qualification that they do not tend to a reproach of the deity, the legal and the naturally lawful cannot clash, for the law of nature forbids breach of contract and therefore the law of nature commands us to keep all the civil law.

This doctrine was objectionable to almost everyone, although for different reasons. "Hobbism" became a term of reproach, and there were few instances of even qualified praise of Hobbes from any English quarter until the nineteenth century. Perhaps the greatest objection was to Hobbes's advocacy of absolute monarchy, but this does not concern us here. Important also in stirring revulsion against his doctrines was his alleged vilification of human nature, the petty role he gave to the law of nature as a sanction of virtuous conduct, and the supreme role he gave to the political sanction for good conduct, to the neglect of other conceivable supports of virtue even in the absence of government.

In reply to Hobbes's claim that only force was an adequate guarantee, or "sanction," of good conduct, his critics stressed, as other inducements to good behavior, love of God, conscience, man's natural benevolence and liking for his fellows, the natural harmony between the interests of man, and the expectation of divine rewards and punishments in this world and in a future world. The moral philosophers to a large extent divided into schools according to which of these they most emphasized. There were probably none, however, who did not appeal to several of these factors, and heavy emphasis was sometimes placed on a particular factor because it was regarded as most neglected, or as most in need of strengthening, rather than as inherently most powerful. Some of the eclecticism was unconscious and involved in self-contradictions. Much of it, however, was conscious and deliberate, either on intellectual grounds or on the pragmatic ground that no conceivable support of virtue should be discarded or overlooked.

The most common objection to Hobbes's doctrine was his insistence on a monopoly of power for the sovereign in the regulation of social conduct. This objection was raised both by those to whom the interests of the Church or of religion were foremost, and by those who cherished the English separation of political power between monarch, Parliament, and the judiciary. One consequence of this was that it made much of eighteenth-century ethical literature, and political literature as well, tend to be misleading to modern readers as a reflection of eighteenth-century attitudes towards the State. Many writers of the time overcompensated for the monolithic role Hobbes assigned to the State by giving little or no attention to the functions of the State as a regulator of social behavior. These writers did not deny that the

State had such functions. They tended, however, to take them tacitly for granted, with the consequence that one could scarcely learn from their writings that there existed public administrators of legal justice, or that England was a mercantilist state. The fact was, however, that, from 1689 on, English thought, and from 1709 on, Scottish thought also, uncritically accepted, when it did not expressly eulogize, the prevailing political, social, and economic institutions substantially as they were. With very few exceptions, and with no exception of first-rank importance before Adam Smith, they had no desire, for instance, that the range of government activities in the economic sphere should greatly diminish. Hobbes himself, writing at a time of civil strife, and zealous for a government strong enough and with a sufficient monopoly of power and of organized influence to maintain internal peace, seemed to write as if his goal was not only an omnipotent but also an omnivorous government. It is reasonably clear, however, that such was not in fact his real intention. So also, Hobbes's critics, in their anxiety to conserve an independent role for the Church and for religion, and to leave to citizens in their capacity as free-will individuals an adequate arena for moral behavior, dealt only casually with the role of the State, although we have no reason to suppose that they wished it substantially altered from its then status.

I can deal here only with a few of the major participants in the discussion of the nature of the sanctions for moral or social conduct.

A number of the major trends in eighteenth-century ethical thought stem from Bishop Richard Cumberland's *De Legibus Naturae* (1672), written as a reply to Hobbes. It had an important influence on Shaftesbury, on Francis Hutcheson, and probably on Adam Smith, as well as on the French physiocrats. To meet Hobbes's doctrine squarely, Cumberland bases his analysis on a state of nature without government, and also deliberately refrains from appealing to religious sanctions in the form of either special interventions or future rewards and punishments. He then argues that, together with the natural liking of men for each other and their capacity for benevolence, God has so ordered the world, including external nature and human nature, that there are sufficient "contingent" sanctions in the shape of temporal rewards for virtue and punishments for vice to make possible a peaceable and tolerable society even in the absence of any civil authority.

Cumberland puts most of his stress on the harmony between rational self-love and benevolence:

> The greatest benevolence of every rational agent towards all forms the happiest state of every and of all the benevolent, as far as is in their power; and is necessarily requisite to the happiest state which they can attain, and therefore the common good is the supreme law.

That most individuals will act on the belief that they can best serve their own happiness by promoting the public good Cumberland rather dogmatically asserts or supports by geometrical analogies whose relevance he takes for granted rather than logically argues. The nearest thing to argument is his assertion that the individual who from "self-condemnation" or because of a "departure from reason" establishes anti-social habits is likely to ruin himself. Such an individual sets other men a bad example which will be highly prejudicial to himself; he increases general suspicion and distrust, whose inconveniences will at some time rebound on himself; he will excite other persons not immediately injured by his behavior, out of regard for the public good and for their own prospective interests, to inflict visible punishment on him in order to restrain other potential malefactors; his immediate victims will seek revenge; he himself will undergo the fear of divine vengeance. As against Hobbes's argument that in a state of nature man has no incentive to consider the welfare of others, he insists that in a state of nature every man has a right to punish and a presumable interest in punishing the crimes of others even if he is not an immediate victim of these crimes. The mutuality of benefit of the institution of private property he claims to be so obvious that it would be recognized even in a state of nature.

> These propositions seem to me to have the greatest evidence, little different from that of mathematical axioms. The good of the whole is greater than the good of a part. The causes which most effectually preserve and perfect a whole or aggregate whose parts mutually require one another's assistance do in like manner preserve and perfect the parts thereof. The aid of those who do not acknowledge such first principles of acting rationally is either not to be sought after or, if necessary, it is to be procured by the assistance of those who do acknowledge them.

This sounds very much like what is now called "the fallacy of composition," which becomes more serious the larger the group involved. One of Cumberland's editors, John Maxwell, expresses his dissatisfaction with the adequacy of this attempt to show correspondence between public good and recognized individual advantage. He comes to Cumberland's assistance with special reference to economic activity, by a line of argument which somewhat anticipates Adam Smith. The essence of it is that through the operation of division of labor all men are dependent on the help of others and in serving themselves are incidentally serving others, so that "the public good is in the greater number of cases most plainly connected with private advantage." What he needed to show, however, was that it was connected with individual private advantage.

Cumberland later has recourse to more empirical arguments, resting in part on psychological considerations, which he in turn bases on physiological and anatomical factors, as well as on introspection. The physiological argument is offered as a buttress to his own introspections. It is in any case a generally overlooked anticipation of the later Hartley—James Mill—Alexander Bain approach to a physiological basis for psychology and ethics.

If Cumberland had stopped here, his work would have constituted a pioneer—perhaps the pioneer—exposition of philosophical anarchism. But toward the end of his book he "demonstrates" by geometrical analogies the necessity of "subordination" in society, if the required "concurrent assistance of every one, by mutual services of very different kinds" is to prevail "with certainty and steadiness" and concludes that from this proof of the necessity of subordination or "government in general" it is easy to proceed to a proof of the necessity of civil government. This can be fully reconciled with his earlier argument only if he is interpreted to believe that a state of nature can be a tolerable state, but that a society living under civil government would be much better.

Two main lines of development of ethical doctrine stemmed directly or indirectly from Cumberland's argument, although each of them also had much earlier sources. One of these lines stressed the role in social welfare of man's instinctive capacity for disinterested benevolence, and came to be called the "sentimental" school. The other stressed the incidental harmony between behavior engaged in from calculated self-interest and the public good, and acquired the label of the "selfish" school, where "selfish" meant, however, merely calculated self-interest.

A major representative of the sentimental school was the third Earl of Shaftesbury, who exercised great and acknowledged influence on later important writers, and was the pioneer expounder of the so-called "moral sense" doctrine, which postulated a psychological faculty, akin to taste, for distinguishing good from evil. According to Shaftesbury man had a "moral sense," an innate capacity for distinguishing virtue from vice. Virtue consisted solely in the exercise of benevolence for its own sake, without regard to temporal or future rewards. Man derives his greatest happiness from the exercise of benevolence:

> Thus the wisdom of what rules, and is first and chief in nature, has made it to be according to the private interest and good of everyone to work towards the general good, which, if a creature ceases to promote, he is actually so far wanting to himself, and ceases to promote his own happiness and welfare.

Man is naturally a social animal; indeed, he is sometimes too much so for the good of mankind, for the "herding principle" is often responsible for social disorder.

While there is no "virtue" without deliberate desire to do good, there is "mere goodness" in human nature which while falling short of virtue operates as a supplement to it in promoting the happiness of mankind, and is necessary for this purpose. Here fall the whole range of self-regarding interests, and especially the economic ones, provided they do not take anti-social forms.

> Wealth and power are the most effectual means, and the most powerful instruments, even of the greatest virtues, and most generous actions. . . . The pursuit of them is laudable, when the intention is virtuous; and the neglect of them, when honourable opportunities offer, is really a weakness.

> Now as to that passion which is esteemed peculiarly interesting, as having for its aim the possession of wealth, and what we call a settlement or fortune in the world: if the regard towards this kind be moderate and in a reasonable degree; if it occasions no passionate pursuit; nor raises any ardent desire or appetite; there is nothing in this case which is not compatible with virtue, and even suitable and beneficial to society. The public as well as private system is advanced by the industry which this affection excites. But if it grows at length into a real passion, the injury and mischief it does the public is not greater than that which it creates to the person himself. Such a one is in reality a self-oppressor, and lies heavier on himself than he can ever do on mankind.

Some passions, like pride, envy, malice, misanthropy, are

anti-social, but these are not natural to man, and put him at odds with himself. Aberrations from virtue are not due to innate viciousness, but arise only from "the force of custom and education in opposition to nature." The degree to which self-interest actually prevails, moreover, is commonly exaggerated:

> You have heard it (my friend) as a common saying, that *Interest governs the world*. But I believe, whoever looks narrowly into the affairs of it, will find that passion, humor, caprice, zeal, faction, and a thousand other springs, which are counter to self-interest, have as considerable a part in the movements of this machine.

Shaftesbury, therefore, although he excluded consideration of rewards and punishment, temporal or future, from "virtue," granted that calculation of temporal gain played a useful part in the routine business of life. It is "philosophy to inquire where, and in what respect one may be most a loser, which are the greatest gains, the most profitable exchanges, since everything in this world goes by exchange."

In the eighteenth century, all those moral philosophers who denied that man was capable of disinterested benevolence either at all or sufficiently to make it a significant factor in explaining socially-beneficial behavior were by their critics assigned to the "selfish school." An important branch of the school found in self-interest, including as such the theological sanctions appealing to self-interest, that is, the hope of future rewards and the fear of future punishments, the only effective and rational support for good social behavior. In the nineteenth century, A. C. Fraser gave to the doctrines of this school the label "theological utilitarianism." These doctrines received their fullest development at Cambridge University in the eighteenth century.

The theological utilitarians were all hedonic utilitarians, inasmuch as they found the sole effective sanction of moral behavior in the expectations of the agent as to its consequences for his individual happiness, happiness being interpreted in terms of pleasure and pain. They insisted that there was no moral obligation on man to act contrary to his nature, that it was natural for man always to seek his own happiness, and that there was therefore no obligation to disinterested benevolence.

The theological utilitarians denied that there was such a thing as an innate moral sense, or innate conscience, to move man to virtuous behavior. The Rev. John Gay said of "moral sense" and the "public or benevolent affection," asserted by Hutcheson to be, like instincts, independent of reason and not requiring explanation, that they were too much like the "occult qualities" of the schoolmen. Edmund Law said with reference to them that "I take implanted senses, instincts, appetites, passions and affections, etc. to be a remnant of the old philosophy, which used to call everything innate that it could not account for; and therefore heartily wish that they were in one sense all eradicated." Theological utilitarianism in its extreme form starts out from the psychological postulate that normal man is incapable of acting except to pursue pleasure or to avoid pain—his own pleasure and pain. In this life, however, rewards often go to the undeserving and the virtuous are often in misery. But Revelation tells us that in a future life there will be full redress for the inequities of this life. Morality thus has sufficient sanctions and is rational, as distinguished from being instinctive or innate.

The most comprehensive and systematic exposition of theological utilitarianism that I have found was by Thomas Rutherforth, professor of divinity at Cambridge University, in his *Essay on the Nature and Obligations of Virtue* (1744). Rutherforth maintains that the meaning of virtue, as derived from common usage, and as distinguished from "natural good," is "that quality in our actions, by which they are fitted to do good to others or to prevent their harm," or "that part [in a man's] behavior, by which he makes others happy." "Natural good" is "that happiness which is enjoyed by himself." It is not in the nature of man, however, to pursue virtue except as it promises to result in good for oneself, and Francis Hutcheson is wrong when he claims that there is an "instinct" for doing good. Rutherforth does not deny that they who say they love virtue really do love it. But he is skeptical. Declaring that "the reader must not expect me to prove, that no man ever acted upon disinterested motives, or that no virtue was ever practiced without some selfish views," Rutherforth cites, to laugh at it, the instance given by Shaftesbury of two lovers who make the ultimate sacrifice, of suicide, rather than violate their marital obligations. They must be presumed to do so, says Shaftesbury, without hope of compensation. for, he asks, "who ever thought of providing a heaven or future recompense for the suffering virtue of lovers?" Rutherforth acidly comments:

> if this sweet enthusiasm occurs, it is not natural. But it is to be hoped, that they [that is, the deists skeptical of an afterlife], who would call these sufferings a virtue and think it our duty to submit to them, will be so kind as to allow there may be a heaven to reward them.

> For whether we follow nature as it appears in the behavior of mankind in general, or attend to the dictates of reason as they are represented in the writings of philosophers, our own happiness is what we must prefer to everything else, and therefore is the only end which we are likely to pursue with steadiness and constancy. Virtue if it should interfere with this end would soon be deserted; or, if it had no relation at all to our good, would be indifferent to ourselves, whatever it might be to other people.

Self-interest confined to temporal goods can go some way toward promoting the general good, especially in the field of economic activity, but does not suffice. This is in accordance with Divine intent;

Thus has the infinitely wise God so contrived the order of things and the constitution of man, that communicating happiness to others is a likely way to procure it for ourselves. But to keep the government of the moral world in his own hands, He seems to have left some cases purposely unprovided for. He has given us in this life so much good as may serve to make us thankful, but not enough to make us independent. He has caused that virtue, which generally produces happiness to those who practice it, should often fail and should sometimes make them miserable.

Since man is obligated to be virtuous only as he can expect to obtain happiness from it, and since there can be no assurance that the practice of virtue will result in temporal happiness, it is only the promise by revelation of future rewards and punishments which makes virtue a duty:

The constant and uniform practice of virtue towards all of mankind becomes our duty, when revelation has informed us that God will make us finally happy for it in a life after this.

The English eighteenth-century theological utilitarians were arguing, explicitly as well as by implication, that in the absence of expectation of reward, on this earth or in the after-life, it was folly to be virtuous. This argument was not original with them. It is imputed to contemporaries by Plato and Cicero. It was adopted by St. Ambrose and by Lactantius. Sir Thomas More attributes it to the Utopians, whether approvingly or satirically I do not venture to say. Leibnitz accepts it, as does Addison in the *Spectator*. Rousseau, in *Emile*, says: "If the Divinity does not exist, only the evil man uses his reason, the good man is insane." It is one of Edward Young's major themes in the *Night Thoughts*. The argument has been used by a host of others, but as in so many other cases, its history does not seem ever to have been investigated.

Theological utilitarianism continued to flourish at Cambridge University into the nineteenth century, where

William Paley's *The Principles of Moral and Political
Philosophy,* which expounded the doctrine, was used as
the textbook in moral philosophy from 1785 on. It was not
dropped from the Cambridge curriculum until the 1830's,
when a revolt against it as repulsive moral doctrine, led by
William Whewell, finally led to its ouster after a reign of
over a century. It seems likely that the revulsion against
theological utilitarianism was in part due to the fact that,
except for its addition of pleasures and pains in the future
life to the pleasure-pain calculus, it was a close counterpart
of Bentham's completely irreligious hedonic utilitarianism.
It seems that the teaching of theological utilitarianism sur-
vived longer in American colleges than at Cambridge University, for I happen to own a textbook edition of Paley's
Principles published in New York in 1855.

It is easy to see how, in the special atmosphere of
eighteenth-century England, theological utilitarianism
could appeal to Anglican divines. In the first place, it
provided an answer of a sort, by its stress on the importance
of religious sanctions for civic morality, to Hobbes's relega-
tion of the Church to a subordinate status under the State
even in religious matters. In the second place, it countered
the deist doctrine that natural religion sufficed to foster a
virtuous society without the need for revealed religion, by
the argument that without the prospect of a future life man
had insufficient motives to virtue and that without the benefit of the Christian revelation man had no assurance of
immortality. Third, by denying the natural goodness of
man in the absence of hope of reward for virtue and by
stressing the lack of correspondence in this life between
merit and reward, it argued for the inadequacy, as a
rational basis for moral behavior, of the moral philosophy
of the sentimental school favored by the skeptics and the
less orthodox. Fourth, by stressing the prospect of a final
accounting in a future life as between the virtuous and the

sinners, it both afforded justification of a kind for complacency about the lack of social justice in the present dispensation, and provided an answer of a kind to the ancient question of how to reconcile belief in a wise, benevolent, and omnipotent author of the universe with the inequitable distribution of this world's goods as between the virtuous and the sinners. This was a good deal for one body of doctrine to achieve.

Unlike theological utilitarianism, which in the eighteenth century appears to have been largely confined to England, theological or cosmic optimism, although important in England, obtained its fullest development at the hands of continental philosophers. It was not, as Leslie Stephen seems to imply, a special doctrine of the deists, but was a common though not universal ingredient of natural theology, which on the Continent, from the time of Leibnitz, went under the label of "Theodicy." The doctrine was often developed without specific reference to social issues, but it had implications for such issues, and it frequently was expressly applied to them.

The first elaborate English exposition of the doctrine was by William King, Archbishop of Dublin, in his *De Origine Mali* (1702). As in the case of other major expositions of the doctrine, King's version of it can be regarded as "optimism" only in a very special sense. It is King's central thesis, not that all is in fact well, but that God could not have prevented or diminished any form or extent of existing evil without there resulting a new evil greater than that which was removed. "Natural evils proceed from the original condition of things, and are not permitted by God but in order to prevent greater." Some of the existing evils are due to the Fall of Man, to his sinfulness. Among these are mortality, barrenness of the earth and the consequent necessity of hard labor for providing food, the subjection of women to men, the pains of childbirth, enmity between men, the banishment out of paradise. Many others are "consequent upon the necessity of matter, and concerning which the Scripture has nothing to induce us to believe that they arose from Sin."

Once man had sinned, all of these evils are according to King beneficial. His treatment of mortality is typical:

> 'Tis notorious how exorbitant bad elections [in the form of spendthrift expenditures] are even amongst the cares and labours which mortals undergo in providing the necessaries of life; and how pernicious strength of parts becomes, when upon a corruption of the will it degenerates into cunning. How much more intolerable then would it be if the fear of death were away.
>
> All then are made mortal, not only thro' the justice, but the goodness of God. For while men are obliged to struggle with hunger, thirst, diseases and troubles, few of them are at leisure to run quite mad, and leap over all the bounds of nature by their depraved elections.

A more famous exposition of theological optimism was Leibnitz's *Theodicée* of 1710. This was on the surface expounded in more cheerful tones, and stressed more the existence of good than the inevitability of evil, so that it lent itself more readily than King's version to vulgarization into a facile optimism. Basically, however, it was perhaps just as pessimistic.

Modern admirers of the poet Alexander Pope have debated *pro* and *con* whether he was a genuine optimist or only a cosmic one on the Leibnitzian model in his famous lines in his *Essay on Man:*

> All are but parts of one stupendous whole,
> Whose body nature is, and God the soul;
> All nature is but Art, unknown to thee,
> All chance, direction, which thou canst not see;
> All discord, harmony not understood
> All partial evil, universal good
> And spite of pride, in erring reason's spite,
> One truth is clear. Whatever is, is right.

In considering the significance for social thought of theological optimism, it is important to keep in mind the diverse lines of argument it could follow. If it found an optimistic explanation for all observable phenomena, or, where it could not do so, explained its failure by the inadequacy of its knowledge, this would lead to complacency towards the *status quo.* If, on the other hand, the "optimism" was really a rationalized pessimism, at least as far as the plight of mankind was concerned, as was substantially the case for King and Leibnitz, this would tend to lead to preaching resignation and passive submission to the miserable and the oppressed. In both cases, although by a different intellectual path, religion could, if desired, easily be used as an "opiate" as far as social action to remedy social evils was concerned.

As the result of his fall, Man's mortal life was a period of probation, in which he would have to undergo many trials and temptations, and his future happiness would depend not only on how he met them, but on his being elected for salvation through the grace of God. The "mathematic glories of the skies" were not matched, therefore, by corresponding glories in the general behavior of man. Both had a common final cause, but the efficient causes were often held to be capable of operating in radically different manners in the two cases. "Natural" behavior was always "good" behavior. But whereas non-rational matter, of sheer physical necessity, obeyed the laws of nature without the possibility of deviation, man, endowed as he was with free will, could deviate from the laws of nature, though at his cost in temporal or future penalties. The possibility of such deviations was part of the divine plan.

Adam Smith, in his *The Theory of Moral Sentiments,* presents an elaborate analysis of what he regards as the immediate psychological factors which govern man's social behavior. By the "moral sentiments" Smith means the sub-

rational feelings, close to the instinctive level, of approba-
tion or disapproval of our own behavior as well as that of
others. As is common in eighteenth-century usage, "moral"
is here nearly synonomous with "psychological," and is not
to be equated with "ethical." Included in the operations of
the sentiments as a sort of mirror apparatus, is "sympathy"
working through a set of at least three "spectators": first,
the "real spectator" or the outside observer manifesting in
some way, perhaps in the guise of a visible "public opinion,"
approval or disapproval of one's own behavior; second, "the
impartial spectator within one's breast" or one's conscience
observing one's own behavior; and third, a hypothetical
external "spectator" for whose possible reactions to our
conduct one relies on one's imagination.

Next comes man's predisposition to conform to the "laws
of nature" as one is aware of them, these "laws of nature"
being the "general rules" of justice which the reason of
mankind has derived by induction from observed experience of the patterns of response of individuals through the
ages to particular situations. Next, there is the appeal to
one's own reason for guidance with respect to how one
should behave. Finally, there are the speculative reason-
ings of the moral philosopher and the commands of legislators with powers of enforcement by punishments and
rewards.

This succession of factors, it is essential to recognize, is
a succession on a *descending* scale of influence and of ethical value. The important thing for the interpreter of Smith
to note is how low down on this scale reason enters into the
picture as a factor influencing social behavior. The sentiments are innate in man; that is, man is endowed with them
by providence. Under normal circumstances, the sentiments make no mistakes. It is reason which is fallible.
Greatest of all in degree of fallibility is the speculative
reason of the moral philosopher, unless the legislator is on

a still lower level. Man, however, tends to attribute to the human reason what is really the wisdom of the Author of Nature as reflected in the sentiments.

In the course of his argument, Smith surveys the mode of operation of the sentiments and points out how often the human rational judgment of them is adverse. But, argues Smith, in such cases it is human reason, not the sentiments, which is in error. Smith's analysis of the sentiments is in form and in fact partly naturalistic and inductive. It is also, however, partly providentialist and teleological, and is so expressly, deliberately, and repetitively. It is in fact an extension, the only systematic and elaborate one I know of, to the subrational behavior patterns of mankind of a type of providentialist explanation which, as I have related at length in my previous lectures, a long line of predecessors had already applied systematically to the physical universe, to the organic world of plants and animals, to animal and human anatomy and physiology, and to the instincts which man shares with the animals.

"Sympathy" is Smith's term for the psychological mode of operation of the whole apparatus of "sentiments." All of this apparatus is peculiar to man, and is subrational. It begins where animal instincts shared by man end, and it ends where human reason begins. It is thus the psychological area between animal instincts and human reason.

In this sub-rational area Smith perhaps even includes the psychological drives which lead man to engage in trade. Man alone engages in barter. As Smith says in *The Wealth of Nations*, "Nobody ever saw a dog make a fair and deliberate exchange of one bone for another with another dog." Smith would have made this a better illustration for his thesis if he had merely said: "Nobody ever saw a dog make an exchange of one bone for another with another dog." Smith finds in human nature "a certain propensity to truck, barter, and exchange one thing for another," but he reserves his answer to the question whether this propensity is instinctive, that is, "one of those original principles in human nature of which no further account can be given," or "whether, as seems more probable, it be the necessary consequence of the faculties of reason and speech." It seems to me that Cannan, in his edition of *The Wealth of Nations*, misses Smith's point when he comments on Smith's reference to dogs, "It is by no means clear what object there could be in exchanging one bone for another." In the first place, it seems to me that some dogs show a preference for marrow bones, while others, not having strong enough jaws to cope with them, would prefer smaller bones. In the second place, Smith is debating with himself whether "the propensity to truck and barter" is an elementary instinct in man, and thus has no conscious objective, or whether it has a rational foundation. That the propensity in its further development in man, its evolution into division of labor, operates with the aid of reason and calculation, Smith does not for a moment question.

To understand the relationship of "sympathy," of the "sentiments," to Adam Smith's economic views as expounded in *The Wealth of Nations* it is essential to appreciate the role Smith assigns, in the operations of "sympathy," to what I will here call, for lack of a better label, "distance," in the spirit of the term "social distance" sometimes used by modern social psychologists with reference to the relations to each other of members of different social classes.

According to Adam Smith the sentiments weaken progressively as one moves from one's immediate family to one's intimate friends, to one's neighbors in a small community, to fellow-citizens in a great city, to the members in general of one's own country, to foreigners, to mankind taken in the large, to the inhabitants, if any, of distant planets. Spatial distance operates to intensify psychological "distance." The concrete nature of the contacts of man with man can also affect the extent to which they involve "distance" in the psychological sense.

For Adam Smith, all of this psychological apparatus is providential; it is designed by God for the benefit of mankind, and it is presumptuous for man, even if he be a moral philosopher, or especially if he be a moral philosopher, to find flaws in it.

> Whatever interest we take in the fortune of those with whom we have no acquaintance or connection, and who are placed altogether out of the sphere of our activity, can produce only anxiety to ourselves without any manner of advantage to them. To what purpose should we trouble ourselves about the world in the moon? All men, even those at the greatest distance, are no doubt entitled to our good wishes, and our good wishes we naturally give them. But if notwithstanding they should be unfortunate, to give ourselves any anxiety upon that account seems to be not part of our duty. That we should be but little interested, therefore, in the fortune of those whom we can neither serve nor hurt, and who are in every respect so very remote from us, seems wisely ordered by nature. . . .

Modern professors of economics and of ethics operate in disciplines which have been secularized to the point where the religious elements and implications which once were an integral part of them have been painstakingly eliminated. It is in the nature of historians of thought, however, to manifest a propensity to find that their heroes had the same views as they themselves expound, for in the intellectual world this is the greatest honor they can confer upon their heroes. If perchance Adam Smith is a hero to them, they follow one or the other of two available methods of dealing with the religious ingredients of Smith's thought. They either put on mental blinders which hide from their sight these aberrations of Smith's thought, or they treat them as merely traditional and in Smith's day fashionable ornaments to what is essentially naturalistic and rational analysis, especially where economic matters and *The Wealth of Nations* are in question. For these writers the teleological aspects of Smith's thought have only nuisance value. This judgment is their undisputed privilege. In my role as historian of ideas, however, I am obliged to insist that Adam Smith's system of thought, including his economics, is not intelligible if one disregards the role he assigns in it to the teleological elements, to the "invisible hand." Since I am under obligation neither to praise Smith nor to bury him, but only to understand him as best I can, I am obliged to give to the role of the "invisible hand" in his total system of thought the weight it apparently had for him.

In his economic analysis Smith operates from the categorical premise that the economic relations between men are in effect fundamentally impersonal, anonymous, infinitely "distant," so that the sentiments, with the one exception of "justice," remain dormant, are not aroused into action. It would not be difficult to follow Smith in this respect when he is considering, for example, commercial transactions carried out by professional merchants of whom one, say, is resident in England and the other in Turkey, and the only communication between them is through equally anonymous intermediaries, or by mail. Smith, however, in his general treatment of the market, although often not when he is dealing with particular cases, writes as if he accepts as realistic the same psychological assumptions when he is considering the relationships of master and servant, landlord and tenant-farmer, employer and employee, as when he is discussing foreign trade.

Let me illustrate by Smith's treatment of the economics of slavery. Smith insisted that slave labor was never as profitable to the slaveowner as would be free labor, under otherwise similar circumstances. Smith conceded, however, that the advantage of free over slave labor could be much less in some climates, and for some types of cultivation, than in others. He explains the survival of slavery by a non-economic bias in favor of slavery:

> The pride of man makes him love to domineer, and nothing mortifies him so much as to be obliged to condescend to persuade his inferiors. Wherever the law allows it, and the nature of the work can afford it, therefore, he will generally prefer the service of slaves to that of freemen.

There is a limit, however, to the economic price slave-owners will pay to gratify their non-economic preference for slavery. Referring in 1776 to a recent emancipation of their slaves by the Pennsylvania Quakers, Smith commented:

> The late resolution of the Quakers in Pennsylvania to set at liberty all their negro slaves may satisfy us that their number cannot be very great. Had they made any considerable part of their property, such a resolution could never have been agreed to.

Another Scottish philosopher, James Dunbar, familiar with *The Wealth of Nations,* apparently found this interpretation of the Pennsylvania Quakers' decision unpalatable. In a book published in 1780, he attributed the decision to much more exalted motivation:

> The late resolution of the Quakers in Pennsylvania to emancipate their negro slaves seems to evidence a degree of pure and disinterested virtue in that people, beyond the example of the most virtuous communities of ancient times.

It seems highly improbable that either Adam Smith or James Dunbar was well informed as to the situation in Pennsylvania. I am sure that Smith commits a serious error of fact in his treatment of the economic man when he describes him as even within the area of strictly economic transactions operating generally or even often as a *purely* economic man. But I share his little faith in the existence in any number of *purely* non-economic men. In any case, what is involved here is primarily a question of fact. By chance, I very recently came across an article by D. D. Wax, published in 1962 in the *Pennsylvania Magazine of History and Biography* and entitled "Quaker Merchants and the Slave Trade in Colonial Pennsylvania." This article reports, on the basis of correspondence files of several Philadelphia merchants of the time, that in part at least the withdrawal of Quakers from the slave trade did have economic reasons, the unsuitability of the Pennsylvania climate for the health of the slaves, the low profitability of slave labor under the conditions of Pennsylvania agriculture, and so forth. This does not suffice to vindicate Smith, but it does perhaps leave him with one leg to stand on.

Another element of vulnerability in Smith's providential system was that by emphasizing the divine origin of the moral sentiments and attributing to them so much power to influence the patterns of social behavior, Smith tied himself implicitly at least to a static or non-evolutionary theory of social psychology. I have found not even a casual reference in *The Theory of the Moral Sentiments* to the moral sentiments being influenced by changes in the physical or political environment or of their being different in different countries or at different stages of history. Here is apparently a genuine lack of harmony between the static character of human psychology as pictured in *The Theory of the Moral Sentiments* and Smith's stress on patterned historical development in his treatment, in his other writings, of economic history, of the evolution of religious thought, and of many other social phenomena.

Finally, I should not close my lecture without some comment on the role of *laissez-faire* ideas in Smith's providential system and in the providential systems of earlier writers. Before the 1750's, *laissez-faire* played no significant role in any of the predominant systems of religious, or ethical, or political thought. Systematic economic thought had not yet really appeared. To most writers of the period, as of earlier periods, government, at least after the Fall of Man, was as natural as any other social institution, and its evolution, when discussed at all, was often treated as a phenomenon as spontaneous, as devoid of human central planning, and as receiving as much guidance from providence, as language, or as the development of knowledge in general. Adam Smith's *laissez-faire* principles were part of a simultaneous appearance of substantially new attitudes toward the role of government in economic matters in England and in France. These new attitudes were a sharp break from all the old systems of thought, and I cannot see that either the physiocrats or Adam Smith had more than very partial success in fitting the minimization of the role of government as a matter of fundamental principle into their own total systems of thought.

Had these writers treated *laissez-faire* as merely an expedient, resort to which was made temporarily urgent by contemporary circumstances and could be supported logically by inductive inference from empirical evidence, it could, I think, more easily have been fitted into contemporary systematic thinking, and have won more recruits from the philosophically minded. The physiocrats, Adam Smith, and later Kant, but not on the whole the major English classical economists, in effect demanded that there be added to the Decalogue a condemnation of governmental interference with the economic freedom of individuals going beyond the enforcement of commutative justice. It took some time before *laissez-faire* attained this status, and it did not retain it for very long after that time. The defense of *laissez-faire* still undertaken in some quarters today is usually not overtly based on providential doctrine or on moral principle but relies on arguments from expediency. This is a much easier task.

IV. *The Providential Origin of Social Inequality*

IN THE PUBLIC ANNOUNCEMENT of my series of lectures I
gave as the title for this final lecture a verse from a hymn:

> The rich man in his castle,
> The poor man at his gate,
> God made them high or lowly,
> And order'd their estate.

A more prosaic title for this lecture would be: "The Providential Origin of Social Inequality."

A word may be appropriate here as to the place in history
of the hymn from which I have quoted. As I will elaborate
on later, the history of ideas relating providence to social
inequality has two major strains: first, a defense of providence in creating social inequality; and, second, a defense
of social inequality as being in conformity with the intent
of providence. The hymn I quote I interpret as belonging
to the second strain, as being a defense of social inequality
rather than a defense of providence, but I am not certain
of this. It has been a common practice of providentialists
in the same breath to defend a social situation by the claim
that it has providence as its final cause and to justify providence in terms of human ethics by appeal to the admirable
social consequences of its decrees; other hymns by the
author of this one show more clearly that she venerated
providence more than she cherished social inequality. In
any case, the author of the poem was Cecil Frances Alexander, the wife of William Alexander, who at the climax of
his career was the Primate of the Anglican Church of Ireland. The hymn was written at some time in the middle
years of the nineteenth century. It had some popularity
and it was included in hymn books of wide circulation. But
it came late in the tradition to which it belonged, an ancient
tradition since the castle with a beggar at its gate appar-

ently frequently appears in old paintings. This hymn is one of the latest in time that I know of the expressions of the providential responsibility for an unequal social stratification. In eighteenth-century England this hymn, no matter which of the two interpretations one gives it, would have been received enthusiastically. When written, however, it probably was a more faithful representation of Irish than of English Anglicanism. In Ireland the rich man in his castle was likely to be Anglo-Irish, a Protestant, and a member of the established Church of Ireland, while the beggar at his gate was almost certain to be of native Irish origin and a Roman Catholic. It was somewhat easier, therefore, for a member of the higher ranks of the Irish Establishment than of the English one to see the hand of providence in the existing social arrangements, since for the Anglo-Irish the social and economic hierarchy corresponded also to a religious and a racial scale of values.

The relevant primary material on the relations between ideas on providence and ideas on social structure is boundless in extent, and almost so in time, but there is a great scarcity of systematic study on a historical basis of these relations. Limitations of time as well as the limitations of my knowledge force me, therefore, to be selective. I will concentrate on eighteenth-century England, but with occasional glances backward, forward, and laterally, to other countries.

An English writer, one John Edmonds, of whom I know only that he was an Anglican minister, in 1761 stated succinctly what made religious-minded men of his time anxious to find a persuasive defense of providence as against those with equalitarian notions to whom the unequal distribution of this world's goods seemed an obstacle to belief in the benevolence and justice of God:

> No one thing hath more perplexed considerate men, in forming their sentiments of the Supreme Being, or been thought more

difficult to resolve, than the seeming very unequal distributions of good among the creatures here in this world; and especially, among the individuals of our own species. Many in all ages have fairly stumbled at it. And it has had on the minds and manners of vast numbers extremely unhappy effects (including a tendency towards loss of religious faith).

One basic and ancient argument in the defense of providence for creating (or permitting) social inequality was that order and civil peace were the great needs of human society, and that hierarchy and subordination were instrumentally essential if order and civil peace were to prevail. This was continually repeated, as a sort of axiom. If it at all needed supporting argument, it needed it only as a reply to those few who appealed to the utopian literature in which common property was treated sympathetically, or to the community of property practiced by Christ's earliest disciples in Jerusalem, or to its acceptance as an ideal and even its adoption in practice by Catholic monastic communities and by various minor heretical sects in both the Catholic and the Protestant worlds. The common reply to references to the sharing of property by the earliest Christians in Jerusalem was to point to the partial character of the sharing practiced there, and to claim that it was an emergency expedient, akin to the regime in a city under siege or on a ship far from a port and short of food. The earliest Christians, as proponents of this view pointed out, were a small group, mostly poor, and living in the midst of a hostile population. What was essential for their survival had little or no bearing for an established and secure community. Against sectarian communism, they argued that it involved isolation from the mass of mankind and thus inability to serve it, that it provided inadequate incentives to individuals to produce and to conserve scarce goods, and that it was consistent with the maintenance of order and with survival only if it operated under some kind of supreme authority which left almost no freedom to the individual to depart in his behavior from a prescribed routine. The argument from the political and economic inefficiency of equality of status and income was capable, of course, of indefinite elaboration stressing the economic virtues of private property and individual enterprise. But this argument, while still awaiting its historian, lies outside the limits I have adopted for these lectures.

Another line of defense of providence for creating or tolerating inequality was that certain kinds of social inequality were phases of a general pattern of inequality in the universe as a whole which were inherently good, and not merely instrumentally good as serving some political or economic ends of human beings and their communities. They were good transcendentally as values of God and were therefore not properly to be appraised by men on the basis of human standards of virtue and of human aspirations. May I point out in this connection that those moderns who take for granted that social equality is of itself a virtue, and that their belief rests on a solid basis of religious tradition, are seriously misreading the history of religious ideas. During most of the recorded history of man's thinking, including his religious thought, it has been taken for granted by most rulers, theologians, and philosophers, that it is only in heaven that man could, or should, expect equality to prevail. Social equalitarianism as doctrine is essentially a contribution of minority and short-lived heretical sects and of nineteenth-century religious and secular thought.

One argument to support the belief that God was not committed to equalitarianism on earth was the claim that he was not committed to it even in heaven. As Sir Walter Raleigh, echoing a long and already ancient tradition, pointed out, God had introduced gradation or hierarchy even among the corps of angels. In the eighteenth century it was occasionally noted that God had dealt out his revelations partially, bestowing them on some but not on other peoples, and on some but not on other individuals. Inequality in the pattern of revelation, inequality in the pattern of social relationships, inequality in the status of individuals in the ecclesiastical, including financial, arrangements of the Church of England, each of these was cited by writers as evidence of the absence of commitment of God to equalitarian principles. One Anglican divine, John Balguy, appealing to God's handling both of revelation and of social inequality on earth, even approached closely to rejecting universalism as one of the qualities of Godhead; universalism is "a levelling rule" which it is an "undoubted fact" that Heaven does not follow. Echoing probably the "Great Chain of Being" doctrine, which I shall comment on in a moment, Balguy declares:

> That variety, distinction, subordination, which are visible everywhere, and prevail all over the creation, as they often conduce to the benefit of mankind, so, whether they do or not, they are sure to promote the beauty of nature, and the perfection of the universe.

These qualities of "variety, distinction, subordination" may when applied to the earth be of benefit to mankind, but this is incidental to their value *per se* as qualities precious to God.

The doctrine of the Great Chain of Being maintains that the universe was so designed as to comprise a complete scale of beings from the lowest to the highest, and a complete range of beings of every possible species, so that it would possess to the utmost possible extent the characteristics of gradation, variety, and continuity. Of all the ideas I discuss in my lectures, this is the only one which, as far as I know, has had its history carefully and comprehensively traced. Arthur O. Lovejoy lavished his unrivaled erudition and craftmanship on this set of ideas in his famous book, *The Great Chain of Being* (1936), a book that set a model for historians of ideas. I can thus deal with the Chain-of-Being doctrine more briefly than might otherwise be appropriate, and shall confine myself to the few but important points at which the doctrine is directly relevant to the relationship between providence and social inequality within civil society.

Lovejoy gives to what he regards as the key principle of the Great Chain of Being doctrine the label "principle of plenitude." Complete "plenitude," I would suppose, would imply not only a complete scale of beings, the utmost variety, and the maximum variety, but that within each category of beings there would be no exact duplicates. Some exponents of the Great Chain of Being idea assuredly did ascribe to the chain fullness in this sense, but it seems to be absent in many formulations of the idea. To the label for the idea used by another writer, "the principle of perfection," Lovejoy objects that the doctrine expounds "rather the principle of the necessity of imperfection in all its possible degrees." I am under the impression, however, that this point was taken care of by at least some exponents of the doctrine by their emphasis on "variety," a term which Lovejoy does not emphasize. Such exponents, with the aid of "the principle of variety" understood as infinite variety, were able to include "imperfections" from other points of view or on the basis of other human criteria of value as part of "perfection" as seen from a more transcendental point of view. In any case, "variety" or "plenitude," understood to mean the providential existence of all possible differences in kind and in status, and accepted as a mark of perfection by transcendental, if not by human, standards, would represent a tribute to God. It would incidentally also provide an avenue to the use of the doctrine to justify on providentialist grounds any observed terrestrial phenomenon, including social inequality and noxious insects, regardless of whether on a human basis of evaluation it worked for or against the temporal welfare of man. Gradation, continuity, a universally pervasive inequality, were essential if the principle of "plenitude" or of "variety" was to receive full application.

Lovejoy finds in Plato the origins of the metaphysic on which the Great Chain of Being idea rests, and he argues that this metaphysic is on a conceptual level which has no contacts with "common sense" reasoning or with empirical observation. He says that, "It was in the eighteenth century that the conception of the universe as a Chain of Being, and the principles which underlay this conception—plenitude, continuity, gradation—attained their widest diffusion and acceptance." He also says that "Next to the word 'nature,' 'the Great Chain of Being' was the sacred phrase of the eighteenth century, playing a part somewhat analogous to that of the blessed word, 'evolution,' in the late nineteenth." For at least the English eighteenth century, this seems to me exaggerated. For many English thinkers of the period, the doctrine rested on grounds too metaphysical and had too small a place in the major orthodox literary traditions of Christian thought, to be congruent to rationalistic or to empirical or to anthropocentric modes of thought. The doctrine, moreover, seemed to leave no place for any idea of progress, to leave no room, except through the violation of providential design, for the extinction of species, whether of plants or animals, since this would involve gaps, missing links, in the chain of beings, and to leave no room for change in the political order, since this would involve either a breach in or an extension of a preexisting pattern of "gradation."

I have found only one eighteenth-century economist who used the Chain of Being doctrine to justify economic inequality, Josiah Tucker, Dean of Gloucester Cathedral, both a clergyman and an economist. A eulogist of commerce and reputedly an active seeker of preferment in the Church, Tucker once felt obliged publicly to defend himself against the charge that he made religion his business and business his religion. In a sermon published by him in 1772, he used the text, Romans IX: 21: "Hath not the Potter power over the clay of the same lump, to make one vessel to honor, and another to dishonor," to support the argument that it was in accordance with his sovereignty for God to assign individuals to places in the social scale as he wished. As justification for the creation of a social scale, Tucker appealed to the doctrine of the Scale of Beings:

> This similitude of the potter and the clay may serve well to illustrate the divine procedure in calling forth into being such a beautiful and infinite variety of creatures one above another in the scale of life. From the mere clod or lump of earth . . . there is a gradation to the vegetable,—the animal,—the human,—and the angelic nature. And were we to survey each of those classes of beings in their subdivisions, we should find as great a variety among the individuals belonging to them.—And as to all these things, who can dispute the potter's right? Or what injustice is due to the clay? It can surely be no wrong to me, that I am not created an angel; nor is it any injury to the brute that he is not made a man.

To this another Tucker, Abraham Tucker, a gentleman philosopher of some note, replied: ". . . the question is not what the clay has a right to expect but what we conceive it likely that a beneficent potter would do, if he knew his vessels capable of enjoyment or suffering according to the mould wherein they were cast." In other words, Abraham Tucker interpreted the Great Chain of Being doctrine according to its traditional use as offering a vindication of the attributes of God on the basis of the inherent merits of the design he had imposed on the universe, and did not accept Josiah Tucker's use of it, to justify on human standards the merits of that design. Abraham Tucker saw adverse implications of the doctrine for the temporal happiness of mankind. Pointing out that those who expound the doctrine "cannot deny that there is an immense gap between the highest rank of creatures and their Creator," he asked why there could not also have been a gap between the bottom of the scale and nothing, so as to exclude all those creatures whose existence meant for them evil, misery, abuse. He questioned the weight put in the doctrine on a dominating divine predilection for unlimited "variety":

> Do they [the expounders of the Chain of Being doctrine] make curiosity a [divine] attribute, and imagine the Supreme Being like some great nobleman, who will have animals of all kinds in his menagerie to divert himself with looking upon them?

The doctrine was unquestionably used by some English eighteenth-century writers as a kind of support of the legitimacy of social inequality, but rarely by important writers on social issues. When so used, it seems to have been as top-dressing or as ornamentation to argument less metaphysical, more realistic, more anthropocentric in character rather than as solid foundation for such argument. Most writers on social issues paid no attention whatsoever to the doctrine. I suspect they regarded it as fantasy.

Lovejoy treats the doctrine as reaching its peak of popularity in the eighteenth century, but also as pratically not outlasting the century. He explicitly cites only Victor Hugo as expounding it, in a poem, in the nineteenth century. Except for sympathetic references to the "principle of continuity," which may be interpreting it not in its Chain of Being sense, but in the sense of the scientific maxim, *Natura non facit saltem*. I have not myself found any nineteenth-century expositions of the doctrine.

The idea of the Great Chain of Being still, however, makes an occasional appearance, even in the twentieth century. Pius XII, who was a great eclectic, in an allocution of 1949 made the point that while the scale of beings in general reveals harmony and order, in man this harmony and order can cease at the point where the unconscious act ends and the conscious and free action begins. In a German Catholic *Handbook of Christian Social Ethics* of 1952 the explanation given of God's creation of things is that all things "may proclaim his greatness and participate in his goodness and riches." No creature, however, can approach God's divine attributes. "And so God created many and various things in order that they might make up as far as possible by their great number and variety for what they lack as individual creatures in the power of representation" of the divine attributes. There is apparently here attributed to God, in the tradition of the doctrine of the Great Chain of Being so great an addiction to variety and plenitude that it leads him to be completely unselective in what he creates. I am sure that the author of this handbook had no intention of continuing or reviving this notion. He probably knew little or nothing of its pagan origin and its long history thereafter.

I now leave the doctrine of the Great Chain of Beings and turn to an examination of the use by intellectuals of the standard belief in the providential government of the world as a means of defense or an apology for an existing social *status quo* involving great inequality as between different sectors of the population in power and in wealth. I take the relevant English literature from the Restoration to about 1776 as the material to be surveyed, partly because it is the literature with which I am best acquainted, but mainly because England from 1660 to the 1770's strikes me as presenting a unique case of a spontaneous union of theologians, philosophers, economists, and intellectuals in general, maintained without serious breach of continuity for over a century and without a single outstanding heretic or dissenter, and dedicated to the justification of an existing social structure and especially of its social and economic inequalities. I shall emphasize the part played in the social

apologetics of the period by the belief in the providential
origin of the stratified social order.

British social thought from 1660 to 1776 was marked by
wide-ranging and intense controversy on theological, ethical, political, and economic doctrine. There was also, however, almost complete unity of expressed opinion with
respect to general social policy bearing on such matters as
class-stratification, the rights and duties of the poor, the
proper location of political power, the functions and
limitations of public alms and private charity.

As I see it, the most plausible explanation of the relations
of ideas to social policy during the period would be somewhat as follows:

First, the intellectuals of the period, whether they were
theologians, moral philosophers, political theorists, or
economists, found it necessary, as thinking men normally
find it necessary, to bring their beliefs and their social-
policy objectives into at least external and superficial
harmony.

Second, given the doctrines and given the policies of the
period, this made necessary some overt logical or rhetorical
"accommodation" between what they professed to be their
doctrines and what they demonstrated to be their policies,
so as to remove any too obvious manifestations of incoher-
ence between them.

Third, overwhelmingly it was doctrine which they accommodated to policy, rather than the other way round.

Fourth, given the posited unity of position with respect
to policy, and the consequent absence of an articulate and
hostile or critical or skeptical audience, it was not necessary
for the intellectuals of the period to strive for unity of ideas,
or to put their logical or rhetorical resources to severe
strain in order to attain an acceptable level of performance
in their attempt to show that their social policy was in

harmony with their doctrinal beliefs, or their doctrines with their particular ideas.

The England I am talking about was in all important respects—its major religious institutions, its government, its wealth, its allocation of political power—substantially the privileged estate, the exclusive preserve, of a small minority of Englishmen: the men of property, and especially the men of landed property, and even more especially, the men of large landed property, and the intellectuals whom they employed or subsidized. For the men of property it was a Utopia realized, a Utopia attained. On the whole, they knew this, but believed that things were as they should rightly be. In any case, they saw no occasion for significant change.

Even after 1776, until well on in nineteenth-century England, no major changes occurred in the location of political power, in national economic policy, in the relations of church and state, in the social or political status of the lower middle classes and of the poor. But the period after 1776 and especially after 1789 was a period of new ideas, of intermittent publication of various political and economic and religious heresies, and of organized anti-aristocratic political agitation. A new radicalism was afoot, stimulated by the success of the American Revolution, by the inflow of dangerous ideas, especially those of Rousseau, from France, and by the impact of the French Revolution. For the first time, the lower middle classes had a press of their own, vigorous, daring, talented, aggressive. For the first time since 1660, conservatism felt itself on the defensive and began to fear the imminence of drastic change.

The period I am specially dealing with, 1660 to the 1770's, was a period of great intellectual activity and achievement, of widespread and intense theological and philosophical controversy. But unlike the periods immediately preceding and immediately following it, the period 1660 to the 1770's was, with respect to critical theoretical examination of the fundamentals of the existing social structure, a stagnant or torpid period, a period of entrenched, unchallenged, and complacent conservatism.

During the same period, they ordered these things differently, if not better, in France, where there was throughout most of the period a steady flow of proposals for radical change with respect to the political frame of government, the relations of church and state, the privileges of the aristocracy of the sword and of the robe, the status of the clergy, national economic policy, and the status of the peasant and of the laborer. The French poor themselves were no more articulate than the English poor. But there were many persons in the higher levels of French society who were ready to plead, sometimes with some danger to themselves, on behalf of the poor, whereas I find it impossible to name for England a single figure comparable to Vauban, Boisguilbert, the Abbé de St. Pierre, Meslier, Helvétius, Linguet, the Marquis d'Argenson, Chastellux, Mably, Morelly, Rousseau, and at least a dozen others who thought France stood in need of major social reform.

All the English writers on whom I am about to report were in agreement on at least one point; either major social evils did not exist, or, if they did exist, major social change was not a suitable remedy for them. For the pessimists, of whom there were very few, changes in social institutions would provide no remedy, for evils were due to the failings of individuals. These could not be erased by civil legislation or even by foreseeable moral reform; and resignation and hope for a happier life in another world were the only resources available to the miserable. For the easy optimists, things were about as good as they could be even in temporal matters.

I turn now to some of the specific applications of Theod-

icy, of theological optimism in its several varieties, to the
social problem. One of the arguments of the Theodicists
was that much of the evil we see in this world is only apparent, not real. This was widely applied to the problem of
poverty. The inequality of wealth, it was argued, was often
not an inequality in happiness, and often inequality worked
to the advantage of the poor, since "to the man tried with
plentiful estates" riches were often a burden, and to the
poor their poverty was often a blessing. This, once again,
is an ancient theme. Plato, in his *Theatetus*, makes Socrates
speak of "the commonplaces about the lack of happiness of
a king or a rich man," and Horace, in the first satire of his
first book of satires, says that the poor ought to rejoice because they are spared the many cares of the rich. As James
Harris remarked in 1751, the limitations of the happiness
obtainable by "both the possession and pursuit of wealth
. . . is indeed the tritest of all topics. The poets and authors
have long ago exhausted it." This, however, is an objection
resting on aesthetic grounds. The important question re-
mains as to whether the proposition is true. It is not for me
to give an answer, but I do find a great appeal in the famous
remark La Bruyère once made after he had found himself
discussing the question as to whether there was inequality
of happiness between rich and poor:

> He who is powerful and rich, and to whom nothing is lacking, may
> well formulate the question; its answer, however, should be left to
> a poor man.

Laymen and clergymen alike provided this kind of comfort to the poor and of peace to the consciences of the rich,
but I will for the time being confine my citations to clergymen. Jonathan Swift, in his *Sermon on Mutual Subjection*,
declared that "great riches are no blessing in themselves;
because the poor man, with the common necessaries of life,
enjoys more health, and has fewer cares, without them."

In his *Sermon on the Poor Man's Contentment,* Swift laid it down as "a certain truth, that God Almighty hath placed all men upon an equal footing with respect to their happiness in this world, and the capacity of attaining their salvation in the next; or, at least, if there be any difference, it is not to the advantage of the rich and the mighty." Lawrence Sterne, in his Sermon, *The Ways of Providence Justified to Man,* insisted that "the poor had advantages over the rich, or at least compensations balancing riches; if the rich had more meat, the poor had better stomachs for digesting it; if the rich had more money to hire good doctors, the poor had less occasion for their help." Given the state of medical knowledge and practice in his time, Sterne might have added that it would not have been an unmixed blessing for the sick, whether rich or poor, to have had easy access to medical care.

In the charity schools operated by the Church of England, the education provided was a limited one, with heavy emphasis on teaching the children the Catechism and the duty of submission to their ordained lot in life. A charity school sermon by Dr. Andrew Snape, representative of many such sermons, cites these characteristics of a charity school education as an advantage which the poor have over the rich:

> The wise Providence has amply compensated the disadvantages of the poor and indigent, in wanting many of the conveniences of this life, by a more abundant provision for their happiness in the next. Had they been higher born, or more richly endowed, they would have wanted this manner of education, of which those only enjoy the benefit, who are low enough to submit to it; where they have such advantages without money, and without price, as the rich cannot purchase with it. The learning which is given to them (without charge) is generally more edifying than that which is sold to others: thus do they become more exalted in goodness, by being depressed in fortune, and their poverty is, in reality, their preferment.

James Foster, one of the few dissenting clergymen whose sermons won the open admiration of Anglican dignitaries, claimed, as one of the virtues of the existence of poverty, that without it "there would not be such opportunities for contentment [in the face of hardship] and a patient submission to providence, as a low and penurious condition affords," and also that without the existence of the poor, the more prosperous would be deprived of the opportunity to display their "benevolent and communicative temper" in all "its proper dignity and lustre."

Another clergyman, John Edmonds, whom I have already cited, in a treatise, *An Illustration of the Wisdom and Equity of an Indulgent Providence,* 1761, argued that the poverty of the poor does not put them in a worse condition than the rich. The labors of the poor give them health. If, however, illness does come to the poor, they should remember that it saves them from the hazards which a tendency to vice or folly can get a man into if he is in good health. Ill-health may thus be for the poor—but apparently not for the rich—a mark of "distinguishing [providential] favor." In any case, when the differences as to riches and poverty "result from different circumstances of birth these may properly be considered as the natural event of the most perfect direction of things, not liable on any account to the least censure."

I will now turn to three laymen, Adam Smith, Soame Jenyns, and Samuel Johnson. Adam Smith in *The Theory of the Moral Sentiments* finds no difficulty in reconciling the existence of poverty, of the inequality of wealth as between rich and poor and of status as between the high and the lowly, with the doctrine of a perfectly ordered world. The rewards of wealth and of grandeur are vain and trifling:

> In the most glittering and exalted situation that our idle fancy can hold out to us, the pleasures from which we propose to derive our real happiness are almost always the same with those which, in an

actual though humble station, we have at all times at hand and in our power.

The pursuit of wealth and power is a mistake for the pursuer; success does not bring real happiness: "In ease of the body and peace of the mind, all the different ranks of society are nearly upon a level, and the beggar who suns himself by the side of the highway possesses that security which kings are fighting for." Nature made no mistake, however, when it implanted in men ambition for wealth. It acts as a stimulus to productive activity. If it be asked, why want more products if men already have all they really need, Smith's answer is apparently that it makes possible a greater population to share in the general happiness.

Smith claims that the moral sentiments, on the one hand, and morality as seen by moralists, on the other hand, differ with respect to attitudes toward the two extremes of status, the greatly rich and powerful, the greatly poor and wretched. Moralists exhort us to charity and compassion for the poor; they warn us against the fascination of the rich. Nature knows better however:

> The distinction of ranks, the peace and order of society, are in a great measure founded upon the respect which we naturally conceive for the former [i.e. "the rich and the powerful"]. The relief and consolation of human misery depend altogether upon our compassion for the latter [i.e. "the poor and the wretched"]. The peace and order of society is of more importance than even the relief of the miserable. Our respect for the great, accordingly, is most apt to offend [the moralist] by its excess—our fellow-feeling for the miserable, by its defect. . . . Nature has wisely judged that the distinction of ranks, the peace and order of society, would rest more securely upon the plain and palpable difference of birth and fortune, than upon the invisible and often uncertain difference of wisdom and virtue. . . . In the order of all those recommendations, the benevolent wisdom of nature is equally evident.

Where indolence is associated with virtue, and industry and application with knavery, Adam Smith concedes that moral sentiments and "the natural course of events" (as ordained by providence) clash.

> Who ought to reap the harvest? Who starve, and who live in plenty? The natural course of things decides it in favour of the knave; the natural sentiments of mankind in favour of the man of virtue . . . and human laws, the consequences of human sentiments, forfeit the life and the estate of the industrious and cautious traitor, and reward, by extraordinary recompenses, the fidelity and public spirit of the improvident and careless good citizen. Thus man is by nature directed to correct in some measure that distribution of things which she herself would otherwise have made. The rules which for this purpose she prompts him to follow, are different from those which she herself observes.

It all comes out all right, however.

> The rules which she [i.e. Nature] follows are fit for her, those which he [i.e., man] follows for him; but both are calculated to promote the same great end, the order of the world, and the perfection and happiness of human nature.

If nevertheless, we still find an undue absence of correspondence between reward and merit, Smith points to the consolation derived from the belief that God "will complete the plan which he himself has . . . taught us to begin; and will, in a life to come, render to every one according to the works which he has performed in this world."

In general, Smith claims, there is no justification for the tears of the "whining and melancholy moralists," such as Thomson of *The Seasons* and Pascal:

> Take the whole earth at an average, for one man who suffers pain or misery, you will find twenty in prosperity and joy, or at least in tolerable circumstances. No reason, surely, can be assigned why we should rather weep with the one than rejoice with the twenty.

Soame Jenyns, drawing upon both Chain of Being and Theodicy material, carried his complacency about the state of society so far that his cosmic optimism became indistinguishable from a sort of cosmic Whiggism. This was more than Samuel Johnson's limited tolerance for foolishness could stand, and he let loose a thunderous blast of reproof and criticism whose continued fame has served to keep alive the memory of the unfortunate Jenyns. It was Jenyns's thesis that the divine plan required the highly unequal distribution among men of riches, understanding, and health, but the equal distribution, nevertheless, of happiness. Poverty, or as Jenyns called it, "the want of riches," was "generally compensated [to the poor] by [their] having more hopes and fewer fears, a greater share of health, and a more exquisite relish of the smallest enjoyments, than those who possess [riches] are usually blessed with." As for the unequal distribution of understanding, including under this education, it also is a blessing for the poor:

> Ignorance, or the want of knowledge and [literacy], the appointed lot of all born to poverty and the drudgeries of life, is the only opiate capable of insuring that insensibility which can enable them to endure the miseries of [poverty] and the fatigues of [drudgery]. This ignorance is a cordial administered by the gracious hand of Providence, of which the poor ought never to be deprived by an ill-judged and improper education. [The ignorance of the poor] is the basis of all subordination, the support of society, and the privilege of the [poor.]

As to health, Jenyns concedes that there are what seem to be unnecessary pains and sufferings. He first invokes the argument from the inscrutability of God's intentions. Then, calling upon Theodicy, he says we must believe that even from this evil good comes, and that "from connections to us inconceivable it was impracticable for Omnipotence" to produce the invisible good without the visible evil. Still further to clear up the mystery, he invokes a Chain of Being argument:

> As we [humans] receive great part of our pleasures, and even

subsistence, from the sufferings and deaths of lower animals, may not these superior Beings [the celestial angels] do the same from ours?

Boswell in his *Journal,* reports Dr. Johnson as once saying:

Sir, I was once a great arguer for the advantages of poverty, but I was at the same time very discontented. Sir, the great deal of arguing which we hear to represent poverty as no evil shows it to be evidently a great one. You never knew people labouring to convince you that you might live very happily upon a plentiful fortune.

What Johnson found most repulsive in Jenyns's argument clearly was his cavalier treatment of the sufferings of the sick poor, and especially Jenyns's suggestion that these sufferings may have been decreed by providence for the delectation of the angels.

Almost alone among English writers of the period, Johnson openly casts doubt upon the validity of both the Theodicy and the Chain of Being doctrines: "as far as *human* eyes can judge, the degree of evil might have been less without any impediment to good. [There is ground for] doubt and uncertainty [about] the scale of existence and the chain of nature."

Johnson objects to Jenyns's "gentle paraphrase" of poverty by "want of riches." He points out that there is much poverty which is

want of necessaries, a species of poverty which no care of the public, no charity of particulars, can preserve many from feeling openly, and many secretly . . . life must be seen, before it can be known. This author and the poet, Pope [whom he has unwisely plagiarized], perhaps never saw the miseries which they imagine thus easy to be borne. . . . [As for myself] the compensations of sickness I have never found near to equivalence.

As to the absence of need of education by those Jenyns had referred to as "born to irremediable poverty," Johnson replies:

the difficulty is to determine when poverty is irremediable, and at what point superfluity [of knowledge for the poor] begins. . . . [Can we know who] are born to poverty? To entail irreversible poverty upon generation after generation only because the ancestor happened to be poor, is in itself cruel, if not unjust. . . . I am always afraid of determining on the side of . . . cruelty.

Johnson ends on a note of anguish: there is much misery, and we are in "dark ignorance" as to its ultimate cause.

I should emphasize that the references I have made to particular statements of particular writers are drawn from a literature of vast proportions. I have selected them for their special interest because of their authorship, or the manner in which they present their ideas, or, occasionally, because of the idiosyncracy of a particular idea which they express. But with the exception of my quotations from Samuel Johnson, they are, I believe, truly representative of the general character of the treatment from a religious or quasi-religious point of view of social inequality by the writers of the period, clerical and lay. The many men who wrote on political and economic issues but did not explicitly use religious argument are another matter. They are relevant to the central theme of these lectures only for the important points that, as compared to writers who appealed to theological considerations, these men were on the whole less disposed to recognize obligations for public or private relief of distress among the "deserving" poor, were readier than were the writers from a religious point of view to blame the plight of the poor on the moral shortcomings of the poor, but they otherwise were no more and no less zealous in defending the existing political and economic inequalities.

There were reasons arising out of traditional religious thought as well as out of notorious fact why the theologians were inhibited from explaining inequality in political or economic status as corresponding to inequality in virtue, piety, or other species of merit. If in these matters there was one traditional postulate of Christian doctrine it was that temporal blessings were not distributed according to merit. It was largely for this reason, the theologians claimed, that a heaven and a hell had been established, so that justice would ultimately be rendered. Alternatively, the providential establishment or toleration of disproportion in relation to merit in the distribution of temporal blessings and hardships was explained as intended to lead mankind to hope of heaven and fear of hell. It was rare but not unknown for theologians to encourage prosperous individuals in the belief that their prosperity was a reward by providence for their merit. But if there were any theologians who ever explicitly stated that social groups or classes prospered or suffered on earth as groups or classes because of their superior or inferior religious or moral merit, and that there would consequently be special places assigned to them, as members of their temporal groups or classes, in heaven or hell, my search in the literature has failed to turn up any authentic specimens. One text along these lines is repeatedly quoted, but it is a statement attributed to the Duchess of Buckingham, a silly and snobbish laic, and should be treated, as it has not always been, as certainly eccentric in its explicitness and probably eccentric even as private thought. The statement is in a letter by the Duchess to Lady Selina, Countess of Huntingdon, a patroness of the then new Methodist sect:

> I thank your ladyship for the information concerning the Methodist preachers. Their doctrines are most repulsive and strongly tinctured with impertinence toward their superiors, in perpetually endeavoring to level all ranks and do away with all distinctions. It is monstrous to be told you have a heart as sinful as the common wretches that crawl the earth. This is highly offensive and insulting and I cannot but wonder that your ladyship should relish any sentiments so much at variance with high rank and good breeding.

It is perhaps within the appropriate limits of a lecture on ideas concerning the relation of providence to economic inequality to comment on an eighteenth-century discussion of the economic relations between rich and poor countries which involved, in addition to pioneering economic analysis, an appeal to providential intent. In this discussion, David Hume, Josiah Tucker, and Henry Home, Lord Kames, were the chief participants. The issue turned on whether, as the result of international trade, poor countries checked the economic progress of rich countries by their low-wage competition, or, on the contrary, rich countries fattened through their trade relations on the further impoverishment of poor countries in somewhat the manner postulated as a present-day fact by Gunnar Myrdal, the distinguished Swedish economist.

As against David Hume, Lord Kames was convinced that providence would not permit the ordinary commercial operations of the rich country to have as a consequence the further impoverishment of the poor country. Tucker was convinced that providence would not have so constituted the order of things that to protect its own prosperity a rich country would need to engage in practices toward poor countries "inconsistent with the fundamental principle of universal benevolence." Both men thus used providentialist argument to support their positions, but they also used economic argument which broke ground for future developments in international trade theory. Tucker made the interesting statement in this connection that if economic analysis of high authority, meaning here David Hume's analysis, should seem to involve a reflection on providence, he would remain convinced that there was a flaw in it:

> For though the appearance of things makes for this conclusion, namely, that poor countries must inevitably draw away the trade from rich ones, and consequently impoverish them, the fact, itself, cannot be so.

This is interesting for its explicit expression of the conviction that where there is apparent conflict, economic thought must yield to providentialist thought.

I have confined myself so far in this lecture to English literature. It would be interesting to compare English doctrine with Continental doctrine, Catholic and Protestant, but even if I were adequately equipped to make such a comparison, time would not permit it. I will, however, in order to compare them with related British eighteenth-century thought say something about Bishop Bossuet's views, in the late seventeenth century, with reference to both the conformity of inequalities in status and wealth with the intent of providence and the impropriety of clerics and citizens finding fault with the *status quo* on any grounds. I not only do not claim, however, that Bossuet, writing in Louis XIV's reign, was fully representative of either seventeenth- or eighteenth-century French clerical or lay opinion in his political and social views, but I would insist that he stood out, even in his own time, in his unqualified defense of absolute monarchy.

Bossuet presented an elaborate defense of the providential character of social and economic inequality that anticipated much of the British eighteenth-century writing on this topic, and does not differ from it in essentials. His defense of absolute monarchy had after 1689 no parallel in English writings, but is not of relevance here. A sharp contrast, however, between his views and the almost universal British views, at least after 1689, is to be found in his denial of any right of the Church, of high ecclesiastics, of aristocrats or philosophers, or of the general mass of citizens, to criticize the existing social order. With respect to the Church, he writes:

> wandering like a stranger among all the peoples of the world, it
> has no particular laws touching civil society, and it suffices to say
> to it generally what one says to individual foreigners, that on what

relates to government it must follow the laws of the country in which it makes its pilgrimage, and that it must revere the princes and the magistrates of these countries. "Let every soul be in subjection to the higher powers." That is the only political commandment which the New Testament gives us. . . . The Church stifles in the depths of the hearts of its members, not only any incipient thoughts of revolt, but even the slightest murmurs of civil discontent. It has constantly taught, both by its doctrine and by its example, that one must endure everything, even civil injustice, through which the justice of God himself is secretly exercised.

This is Erastianism and Gallicanism, of a kind then prevalent in France, but carried to extremes which had few if any parallels even in seventeenth-century France, and probably none in eighteenth-century France. The English eighteenth-century defense of the *status quo* was not at all comparable: in the first place, it was a different *status quo* from the French one; in the second place, the English defense was itself an appeal to public opinion based on the supposed moral and social merits of the *status quo*, not an automatic defense of the religious, moral, and economic legitimacy of whatever an absolute monarch should decree.

I must now say a few words about the fate of providentialist doctrine after the eighteenth century, in order not to end my lectures too abruptly as far as chronology is concerned. I will use one key figure, William Whewell, the most effective expounder of providentialist thought before it had to cope with the problem presented to it by the shock of the Darwinian doctrine of the descent of man by natural processes from lower forms of life.

William Whewell, scientist, philosopher and historian of science, moral philosopher, theologian, economist, among other things, was in the early nineteenth century a convinced and assiduous exponent of the role of providence in physical and social phenomena. He denied that, as science advances, the concept of final or providential causes recedes in acceptability. Writing in 1845, he cited as an example of the contrary the history of physiology. He claimed that "in that science the Doctrine of Final Causes has been not only consistent with the successive types of discovery, but has been the great instrument of every step of discovery from Galen to Cuvier." The only adjustment of theology to new scientific discovery he conceded to have proved necessary, or at least expedient, had been a shift from providentialist explanation of particular facts in terms of "special interpositions" to consideration "of design as exhibited in the establishment and adjustment of the laws by which particular facts are produced." There was good reason, he affirmed, and I interpret him to mean by this good scientific reason, to believe that all the laws of the universe "are adapted to each other, and intended to work together for the benefit of its organic population, and for the general welfare of its rational tenants," that is, of mankind. These were not new ideas, but Whewell gave them a new emphasis. The role of providence is generally to be looked for not in particular events but in the general patterns of events and of their interrelationships, that is, in the modes of operation of the laws of nature. When combined with the rejection of literal interpretation of passages in the Scriptures referring to natural phenomena, this made possible uninhibited scientific research and the development, *ex post,* of providentialist explanations of the new discoveries, accompanied by a tacit abandonment of all earlier providentialist explanations of natural phenomena which the march of science had made untenable for scientists.

On one matter, however, Whewell made no concessions from previous providentialist doctrine, namely, on the origin of man. In 1853, or just a few years before he would have been obliged to cope with Darwinism, he declared: "We know, even from the evidence of natural science, that God *has* interposed in the history of this Earth, in order to place Man upon it." He rejected the notion that there were beings resembling man in intelligence, morality, and religion on other planets and expressed disapproval of even entertaining the notion as a speculative one. "God has found it worthy of Him to bestow upon man His special care, though he occupies so small a portion of time; and why not, then, although he occupies so small a portion of space?" To the argument that this implies "waste" by providence of other planets, he replied: "Is waste of this kind considered as unsuited to the character of the Creator? But here again we have the like waste, in the occupation of the earth."

Post-Darwinian providentialist thought accommodated itself to Darwinism by accepting the evolutionary process as a newly discovered manifestation of the majesty and the beneficence of providence. A measure of teleology still survives even in professional scientific literature, although in a somewhat disguised vocabulary where the wisdom of nature, or the wisdom of the body, or "homeostasis," act as substitutes for the wisdom of providence, or of God. Today, however, it is the providentialistic natural or social scientist rather than the positivistic one who is on the defensive. As the result, moreover, of the advent of Christian Socialism, of Social Catholicism, and of the Social Gospel, and of the social forces which had given rise to these movements, such providentialism as survives has almost wholly ceased to be a defense of the social *status quo.*

In conclusion, I will once more attempt a definition of and an apologia for the role of the historian of ideas. It is a modest role. It does not include tracing the social consequences of the ideas which men generate or adopt, but accepts responsibility only for tracing their filiation through time and their relations to other ideas. If one should ask what profit, beyond the satisfaction of curiosity, knowledge of the history of ideas brings, I would not claim much more for it than that by helping us to understand the mental processes of our predecessors it helps us to attain humility with respect to the validity and the durability of our own ideas. I would not deny that, if the study of the history of ideas were to become a mass phenomenon, one result might be a general weakening of convictions, and that this might not be a "good thing." The addicts of the history of ideas, however, are certain to remain few in numbers, and they may perhaps have a claim to toleration on the ground that they have a providential role as a weak counterforce to dogma ruling by inheritance and not by merit and to undue attachment to one's own new ideas through *hubris* or intellectual arrogance.